Contents:

Acknowledgements

As editor of the interviews I am grateful to all of the contributors and to the students who patiently conducted the interviews.

To the young 14 year old students from what was then Guthlaxton College, who began the whole process in 2013, thank you for being brave. To Ashleigh Gibby, Sam Bott, Haris Majeed, Muhammad Ali Musani, Lucy Thompson, Katie Downes and Sophie Clayton.

To the many students from the University of Leicester who spent many hours volunteering with the project I thank Aldo Bader, Uche Ugwu, Vicky Barnes, Eliet Sipos, Becky Mason, Christina Marangou, Siqi Liu, Beth Shelton, Clare Howe, Heidi Turner, Fengyan Wang, Aasiyah Abdulsalam, Tapani Pratumsuwan (who we all know as Preme), Holly Carolan, Fiyin Bakare, Qian and Lucy. I hope that I haven't left anyone out of this extensive list. Thank you to the University for adding me to the volunteering section of the student opportunities site.

In particular I must thank the students from Leicester College who put all of our words and pictures into publishable format and even improved upon our research. To Anna Babinska, **Hannah Benyon, Masimba Muganiri and** Nikola Malecka.

Also to the Heads of Departments at the Leicester College, Matthew Poynton, Print Production Supervisor; Nick Ruhl, Program Leader FD Graphic Design and E-media; Nathan Smith, Module Leader Graphic Design and E-media; Sebastian Buccheri, Module Leader Graphic Design and E-media who all had the foresight to take the project on and made it all possible.

To Age UK Oadby and Wigston for hosting the lunches and entertainments which the contributors attended and enjoyed. Also for allowing me to have the time and space to complete the enterprise.

Most importantly, thank you to all of the people and their families whose interesting and often fascinating, entertaining stories fill these pages.

Finally, thank you to the readers for wanting to read these interviews and hopefully for encouraging others to buy a copy of the book, to raise even more funds for Age UK Oadby and Wigston to help to keep them going for another 50 years. To learn more about the history of this wonderful charity please see the time line featured in the Appendices.

Anne Coulstock 2017

Bell Street Infant's School. Built in 1873 this was the first Wigston Board School after the passing of the 1870 Education Act and was a typical Victorian Structure. A two-storey building was later added on the Frederick Street frontage. The whole site is now occupied by Sainsbury's supermarket.

This school was attended by many people in this book.

FRANK RAYMOND
ADCOCK

Frank was born on 21st August 1918 at home. Frank's father was called William and his mother was Sally Dexter before she married William. Frank's sister, Dorothy, was 11 years younger than him. The family lived in Beaumont Street in Oadby in a terraced house with no bathroom. They probably had a tub in the kitchen but Frank doesn't remember too much about this.

The school which Frank attended was Sandhurst Street School but it isn't there any longer. Frank stayed at school until he was 14/15 when he left to become a trainee mechanic in Rowley's factory. When he was about 16 Frank had a Coventry Eagle motor bike and he admits to being a bit of an "idiot" on it. He wasn't known for speeding because it wouldn't go very fast. When he was 18 the family bought Frank a car so that he would be safer. It was a Morris Minor which didn't get much use because Frank couldn't afford to buy the petrol.

When he was 17/18 Frank got another job where he was a qualified mechanic. He stayed there until he was 20 when he was called up to the Army. He joined Royal Army Service Corps. and was sent straight off to France. Frank's Dad had the car then as Frank wasn't able to use it much. Frank stayed in France until he was shipped out of Dunkirk, travelling to Egypt where he spent the rest of the war. He was in the No1 Pontoon Bridge Company.

Frank doesn't remember any hardships in France but he does remember that when the Germans arrived, in the area he was stationed, they were better equipped and so were more successful than the British. His memories are of being very scared especially when he was on the beaches of Dunkirk waiting to be evacuated. It was very scary being machine gunned for 2 or 3 days until he was finally shipped out. He remembers lots of machine guns and noise; lots of lives around him were lost and this has made a big impact on Frank. Frank and his friends managed to get off the beaches relatively quickly and were sent to Egypt.

NB. Historical reports of the time show that the flotilla of 'Little Ships' evacuated 338,000 soldiers, from Dunkirk to Ramsgate, over a period of ten days. 40,000 men were left behind on the beaches.
The chaos during that time was dreadful for the desperate men who had to wait under fire and amongst minefields not knowing if they would survive.

Frank wasn't in England for VE Day as he was still in Egypt so he missed any celebrations. The war didn't finish for Frank until 1946. He spent the time in Egypt as a vehicle mechanic and driver. (The photo on the title page was taken there.) He was able to visit Alexandria and Cairo but didn't do much sight-seeing. Frank would prefer to keep quiet about what he did with his leisure time! He admits that Cairo was "interesting".
In 1946, at the age of 28, Frank travelled by train through France back to England and he was de-mobbed in Northamptonshire. He remembers that the suit that he was given to wear instead of his uniform was dark grey, the same as all of the other soldiers, but it fitted very well. He spent a year in Kidderminster working in a carpet factory. Frank returned to Beaumont Street, Oadby. The family had moved across the road to a nicer house with a bathroom and indoor toilet. His sister, Dorothy, was in her teens by then. Frank went to work at Wildt, Mellor Bromley as a fitter and stayed there until he retired aged 63. His retirement payment was used by Frank and his wife to have lots of enjoyable holidays. Dorothy married and lived in Oadby until her death.
Frank met his wife, Marjorie when he was on leave from the Army in Kidderminster before his de-mob. Frank and his wife were married in 1947 and went to live in Oadby.

4

They had one daughter, Gill. Frank's memories of his wife are that she liked to dance. As Frank wasn't keen on dancing he would go for a drink instead. Marjorie was diagnosed with breast cancer and suffered for a short period of time before going into hospital, where she died quite quickly.

Gill was also diagnosed with breast cancer and she died during 2002.

The two deaths were very hard for Frank to deal with and he struggled for a while. He began to visit the Bassett Street Centre, in South Wigston, for his lunches and for some social activity. Although the Centre only offered meals Frank was able to make lots of friends.

In 2001 Frank moved into a warden controlled block of flats where he has his own rooms. He has a kitchen but is much happier to visit Age UK Oadby and Wigston every day, Monday to Friday, for his lunch. He enjoys living on his own and likes to keep himself to himself but knows that people are there if he needs them.

Frank is a popular man at the Centre and still enjoys a life surrounded by his ladies.

He recently celebrated his 97th birthday with a special cake and lots of fun and laughter.

To Celebrate the Life

OF

Frank Raymond Adcock

21st August 1918 - 28th June 2016

South Leicestershire Crematorium, Countesthorpe

Monday 11th July 2016 at 12.00 noon

AVIS JOYCE
AMBLER

I am writing these notes based upon the memories of the family and friends of Avis Ambler. Avis was, for many years, a close friend of Florence Drage.*

Avis Boaden was born, on 27th June 1926, in Castle Cary in Somerset. The family moved to Pewsey in Wiltshire in 1931. The family consisted of her parents and Avis with her brothers and sisters, Bill, Celia, Denise and Edward. Avis also had two step-sisters much later from her father's second marriage. Pamela and Angela were born when Avis was an adult. Avis attended Grammar School in Marlborough where she enjoyed academic success as well as being a part of the school community. She also became Head Girl, Sports Captain and was a co-editor of the school magazine.

Although Avis moved away from Pewsey when she left school at 18, she was still very close to her brothers and sisters. Family was very important to Avis throughout her life including Pamela and Angela. Friendships also tended to be lifelong and she was still exchanging cards and news with contacts in Pewsey at Christmas 2014.

From 1944 or so Avis spent approximately a decade in different places around the UK and abroad. Wanting to play her part in the war effort she followed in her sister Denise's footsteps and volunteered for the Wrens. She was interviewed in Salisbury and was told that she needed to receive her training at Tullichewan Castle at Balloch in Scotland. She lived in a camp of Nissen Huts which had been originally occupied by American soldiers.

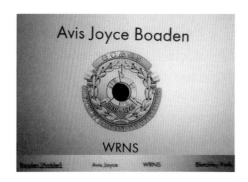

See chapter on Drage Florence

Alongside the other new recruits Avis received a fortnight's training and was then asked if they wanted to stay. They were interviewed and she was asked about her interests and hobbies. They were not told what the job would be but Avis got the definite impression that she would be working in the country and even possibly underground. In other words, Avis believed that they would have to make their own amusements away from the bright lights. She had come straight from school and was used to being told what to do and so she did not even query any of this. She remembered getting up very early in the mornings and cleaning out the 'lats'. Clearly a very memorable time! After the initial training Avis spent two weeks at Wesley College in Leeds; killing time before going on to live at Woburn Abbey, whilst working at Bletchley Park. Here she shared a large bedroom with others so began to get used to living closely with others and presumably setting the pattern for her later concerns with tidiness.

Avis had been interviewed for what she was told would be a 'special role' and was posted to Bletchley Park in August 1944. She worked in Block F, Mr Newman's section, as part of the intelligence operations. Avis worked in shifts at Bletchley Park, arriving after a journey of half an hour in a wartime vehicle with hard wooden seats. The hours were split into watches, each of which lasted for a week; 8am – 4pm, 4pm – 12pm and 12pm – 8am. Avis recalled on one occasion sharing the transport with a dreadful smelling soup which was very off-putting. Even as an eighteen year old Avis took very seriously her oath not to divulge anything about her work. She possibly told her family that she was working in an office. It transpired later that her younger brother, Edward who was in the Royal Signals knew about Bletchley Park and may even have benefited from their work. In 1945 Avis was moved to Gayhurst Manor and was eventually made redundant – a word which she had never heard before.

She believed that it was probably 'last in , first out'. Her work was something that she kept secret from her family and friends for over 50 years until the media focus finally persuaded her to share her memories with her grown up children. Despite being a very sociable person Avis had a reticence about certain things and was certainly able to keep a secret. The family enjoyed a visit to Bletchley Park with Avis and were able to discuss with her the time she spent there. They stood "amazed" in front of the Colossus machine that she had worked on. Avis kept in touch with fellow Wrens and as an active member of the Wrens' Association she often drove them in a mini-bus to Portsmouth for regular events. Some of the work which Avis was involved with in the far east has remained a secret and she has steadfastly refused to talk about the details.

Code-breaker's secret war effort

WAR EFFORT: Avis Ambler, left, as a Wren

BY **PETER WARZYNSKI**

TRIBUTES have been paid to a wartime code-breaker who later became a teacher in Leicestershire.

Avis Ambler helped the war effort with her work at Bletchley Park, Buckinghamshire, home to mathematical genius Alan Turing and the machine he built and used to break the Nazi's Enigma code.

The base employed thousands of people during the war. Avis was an operative in Block F – using the Colossus machine to decrypt German teleprinter ciphers.

But the mother-of-three, who died this week, aged 88, kept her work secret until a few years ago.

Now, her son, Nick, has paid tribute to his mother and the work she did at the

intelligence headquarters. He said: "We had no idea. It was only when the Enigma film with Kate Winslet came out in 2001 and the story became more widely know that she made the decision to tell us.

"I remember her saying one day 'I was involved in that', but I didn't really pay much attention at first.

"The full realisation was when we went on a family day out to Bletchley Park and she showed us the Colossus and a big book of names – and she was in it."

Avis was born in Somerset in 1926. She moved to Oadby in 1960, where she stayed for the rest of her life, working as a teacher at Wigston Waterleys Primary School.

The Leicester City season ticket-holder, who became hooked on the Foxes in her early 80s, was picked to work at Bletchley Park after joining the Wrens.

"Somehow they found out she was good at crosswords," said Nick. "Once there, they gave them a bit more explicit detail and said anyone who wants to leave now can do so.

"Quite a lot of people left, actually, which was surprising."

In 1944, Avis joined about 600 people at Bletchley Park, but was never given any more information than she needed to do her job.

Nick said: "People like my mum only ever saw a tiny part of the whole operation – they worked on one slip of paper at a time and weren't

allowed to talk to the person next to them."

When the war ended, Winston Churchill destroyed everything associated with the code-breaking at the top-secret HQ.

"Her understanding was that she would never be able to talk about it," said Nick.

"She saw what Churchill did and assumed she would have to take everything she knew to her grave."

Nick said his mother remained connected to the Wrens throughout her life and was active in the Wrens Association.

She was also a keen ornithologist and a volunteer at the Oadby branch of Age UK.

Her funeral will be at St Peter's Church, in Oadby, at midday on Thursday.

Reproduced by kind permission of the Leicester Mercury.

(Following her death in February 2015 the Leicester Mercury printed a report of her amazing life and work during the war years and we have permission from the newspaper and her family to reproduce the article.*)

Avis spent one of her holidays cycling in northern France with her great friend Meg. When they returned home they decided to enrol for training as radio mechanics. They worked on naval aircraft in Scotland and this is where Avis met her future husband Bob Ambler. Avis was then posted to the south coast of England. She helped to make up the daily codes used by the Royal Navy. The distance from Scotland, and Bob, caused a few problems but they arranged to travel halfway each so that they could meet up between postings. In 1952 Avis was offered a a job at the new GCHQ at Cheltenham but she chose instead to marry. The new family moved up to Sheffield where the children Nick, Jacqui and Richard were born in quick succession. They moved to Leicester in 1960 when Bob got a job with the National Coal Board office. Avis enjoyed living in a modern house and loved working on the garden at their home in Oadby. When the children had all started school Avis enrolled on the teacher training course at Scraptoft College where she shared the travelling with Florence Drage. They both worked at Waterleys Primary School when they qualified, and made enduring friendships with the staff including Kate and Carys. Avis always had an interest in nature and she developed an environmental room at Waterleys. Her commitment led to carefully incubating and hatching chicken's eggs each year to the wonder of the children.

The years that followed were taken up with the routines of work and family life but always punctuated by a three week family camping holiday abroad. The family travelled all over Europe, pitching the big blue tent, but only after the 'lats' had been inspected and approved! Clearly a life-long lesson, learnt when she was young. In 1979, after the children had left home, Avis and Bob separated and she moved into her own home in Oadby. She created a garden to her own design as well as a comfortable home where she was able to keep everything "ship-shape" the way she liked it. The visiting family soon learnt to adapt to the house rules and knew that the breakfast things would be laid out the night before and that washing up would never be left in the sink! Her neighbours in Oadby became good friends and they encouraged her in a whole host of activities outside the home, particularly after she retired in 1984. She joined many groups including the Business and Professional Women's Association, the Arts Group, the RSPB, the Literary and Philosophical Society and she continued her activities with the Wrens Association. Avis was also a volunteer with Age Concern Oadby and Wigston and as a Trustee she helped to guide the charity through it's new life as Age UK Oadby and Wigston. She volunteered in the coffee shop and spent many valuable hours as an enthusiastic supporter of fund-raising events. Eventually she had to retire from the voluntary work but remained as a loyal customer at lunchtimes. Avis also enjoyed holidays all over the world including many bird-watching holidays with her sister Denise. Avis was also a stalwart Leicester City supporter, attending matches with her friend Peggy and a flask of tea.

Not surprisingly Avis was also a proud Mum and took delight in watching her children grow up and fly the nest. Nick settled in Bristol, Jacqui in Bradford and Richard in Brisbane, Australia. Towards the end of her life these distances became a problem for Avis, especially as she had to give up driving. She was therefore delighted when her grand daughter came to the University of Leicester. They were able to go shopping and out for trips in Liz's car.

Avis had a diagnosis of colon cancer at this time and walking became increasingly difficult. After her operation it was decided that she would recuperate with Bob in his bungalow in Bradford. Avis accepted this offer despite the fact that this meant going back up to the "frozen north" again. Avis had become very independent and was more used to giving support rather than receiving it. The surprise was that she enjoyed it as quite a variety of healing was taking place. Bob could be found cooking meals for Avis for the first time and took her advice on how to keep things neat and tidy in the bungalow. Bob in turn plied Avis with wine at lunch time and they were observed giggling and then dozing together on the sofa on more than one occasion. For her part, Avis could not praise Bob highly enough for the care that he took of her and when she eventually returned home he drove her back to Oadby. Sadly Bob had a fall soon after this time and this resulted in his death.

When Avis became ill again she was helped by the enduring support of many friends including Florence, Margaret, Gill and Brigid. Her support group also managed to keep her garden under control and helped with the shopping, cleaning and hairdressing. They enabled Avis to stay in her own home and maintain her independence. Eventually her family were also grateful to the staff at the LOROS Hospice and in particular for their care during her last days. They were gratified to know that Avis, who had given so much to others over the years, was the recipient of so much kindness and dedication when she needed it most.

Most of the above is taken from the eulogy which Jacqui gave for her Mum at the funeral and she closed by saying " Avis, you have been an example to us in commitment, friendship, self-discipline and endurance: we are so proud of you."

BRADSHAW

Pam was born on 15th March 1938 at the Bond Street Hospital, to Sydney Freer and Gladys (nee Gardner). At this time Sydney and Gladys lived at one of the Tenrow, on Station Road, where the new doctor's surgery is now. This was a row of terraced houses which all shared a long back yard. They all used the same three cold water taps and shared the five outside toilets between them. Pam remembers the smell and the rats.

However, she also remembers playing happily with her neighbours and friends in the communal yard - Whip 'n' Top and marbles were favourites. Pam had a sister, Edna who was born in 1930. When Edna was two years old she was diagnosed as having a dislocated hip.

This would have happened at birth but it wasn't recognised. Edna spent many years in a spinal carriage, a bit like a box pram, and wasn't able to start school until she was 7 years old.

Edna in her spinal carriage

Uncle Dick, Uncle Roy, Sydney, Gladys, cousin Lily, Aunty Alice, Denis

During this time she spent two years in hospital at the City General. Although she was able to attend school she continued to limp for the rest of her life. Edna married Derek and they have a daughter called Julie. Julie is a nurse and she and her husband, Paul have a daughter called Ellen.

Pam, and her sister, both attended Bell Street Primary School (replaced by Sainsbury's now) and then moved to the National School and finally the Board School which was later called the Secondary Modern School, until a new school was built to replace it, later known as Abington High School and now called Wigston Academy.

Pam enjoyed many sports, especially netball. She and her friends enjoyed the social life of school. Pam remembers that the Headmaster of the Board School was Mr Bob Kind. (Uncle to Alan Kind) Other memorable teachers were Mr I. Jones, who taught geography and Mr E Jones, who possibly taught maths and English. Miss King and Miss Deraeve both taught sports but the most strict teacher was Mrs Outridge. She taught needlework and is remembered by many people who attended the school at this time. Although Pam has fond memories of school she "wasn't overly enthusiastic at the time". She did enjoy geography, history and spelling but was far less keen on dramatics!

Pam left school aged 15 and went to work in a hosiery factory called Bradleys which was on Clarke's Road. Her first wage was just over £2. The job was enjoyable particularly due to the social aspect. She stayed there until she was 18 when she moved to Clarida on Bell Street. Both of these manufacturers made 'fully fashioned' ladies knitwear. This term was used to describe knitwear which was made to fit and would have been more expensive than other garments. Pam worked at Clarida until she was 23 years old.

During this time Pam's family had moved from the 'Tenrow' to a council house on Elizabeth Crescent. Council tenants were not allowed to keep animals but the family owned some chickens so they had to find a new 'home' where they could still look after them. A man who had been at school at the same time as Pam lived in a house with an orchard so they were able to take the chickens there and Pam visited them to feed and look after them. The 'man' was called Malcolm and although he and Pam had not talked when they were at school it didn't take long before they were courting. Malc had returned from his National Service in 1957 where he had been to Cyprus. He and Pam began their courtship in 1958/9.

Before his National Service Malc had worked at Corah's in Leicester and he was able to return there when he returned to England and left the army. Malc was made redundant in 1988 and the factory closed soon after.

When Pam and Malc were courting they usually went to the pictures as that's all there was in Wigston. She remembers that the prices were different for different seats. At the front the seats cost 1shilling (5p), in the centre they were 1/6d (approximately 7p), at the back they cost 1/9d (approximately 9p) and to sit upstairs the price was 2shillings (20p). There was also a Saturday morning 'rush' which cost 3d (approximately 0.5p).

Pam and Malc were married at the registry office when it was opposite the Cathedral. Pam wore a blue suit with white accessories. She had a white bunny wool hat with white shoes and blouse. Malc's Uncle Norman and brother Tony, were the witnesses.

Andrea was born in 1958 and Andrew in 1962. Andrea is now a housekeeper for families and 'lives in'. At the time of the chat Andrea is living in Salisbury. Andrew is married to Charlotte and they have two children. Riley was born in 2003 and Megan in 2004. Andrew worked at Corah's when he left school but more recently he was made redundant just before Christmas 2013. He now works for Technical Surfaces making plastic grass. Charlotte was made redundant at the same time and now works in an office at the Meridian Business Park. Riley loves sport and plays rugby for South Leicester Rugby. Megan is a very creative young lady and loves making things. She and Riley raised money for Age UK Oadby and Wigston during the summer holidays by demonstrating, making and selling 'Loom Bands'. They raised a whopping £60!

Megan and Riley

Pam and Malc had moved into a council house in Wigston in 1966 which they were able to buy in 1985. This is a source of pride to Pam and she and Malc love to garden as well. Malc has an allotment where he grows a variety of vegetables.

Pam and her family often went on holiday in a caravan to Mablethorpe and later to holiday flats in Newquay. Pam liked the scenery where they would go for walks and play on the beaches.

Pam then worked at home using a small knitting machine to produce hand flat knitwear. This was helpful as each of her children were born and she was able to stay at home with them. As the children grew up Pam moved to working at The Horse and Trumpet' where she was able to take the children whilst she was cleaning. In 1977 Pam was working at Measom Freers in Wigston making plastic products such as bottles, scoops and 'Red Noses'. She remained there until she retired in 1998.

Some of the most important dates in the diaries of both Malc and Pam are the home matches of Leicester City Football Club. Malc has supported them since 1948 and Pam joined him in 1966. Pam particularly enjoys the banter with Alan Birchenall who they have watched as a player and current Ambassador for LCFC. Malc and Pam both make the matches a priority in their lives and in this year (2016) of Premiership Champions their loyalty has been more than rewarded.

In 1996 Malc was 60 and to celebrate their children treated them to a holiday in Cyprus. Malc found many happy memories and it was especially good as there was no fighting any longer.

For Pam it was the first time that she had flown to a holiday destination. They have been back three times now. Holidays in Kefalonia have also been important to Pam and Malc after Malc's brother recommended it to them when he, Geoffrey and his wife Linda, had visited for a holiday themselves.

In 1988 Pam met her friend Moya* when they both worked at the factory. Pam and Moya have remained friends since and both support Age UK Oadby and Wigston.

Pam had watched the building of the Centre for Age Concern (now Age UK Oadby and Wigston) in Paddock Street so that when she retired she came to the centre for coffee. She has been visiting ever since. Pam has volunteered in a variety of situations at the centre, currently working in the shop she has been the escort for the mini-bus and Pam has also supported the fund-raising efforts of the volunteers. As well as holding a stall for many of the fairs and celebrations which raise vital money for the Centre. Pam and her friend Moya are the organisers of the 'Big Knit' which collects hand knitted little hats for 'innocent Smoothie' bottles in supermarkets across the UK. Targets are set each year and currently they are collecting 10,000 hats from the enthusiastic knitters of Wigston. Pam has also been a Trustee for the charity since 2014. Thanks very much for all of your hard work Pam.

See chapter on Moya Harratt.

DEREK
BUTT

Derek was born at home on the 14th August 1935, in Portsmouth and is the eldest child. He lived with his Mum, Nelly (need Barrett) and his Dad, Leslie.
His sister Rita was born 10 years later. Derek's middle name is also Leslie, after his father.

As a child Derek remembers growing up living directly outside the Royal Marine Barracks and has a vivid memory of the gun on top of the tower used for protection against the Germans. Derek's father was a fireman so was heavily involved in the war. Derek remembers one specific day when a bomb exploded locally and obliterated about five roads. Derek's father's colleagues told him not to put himself in danger by walking home but he was determined to see his family, fortunately he made it home safely. Derek and his mother were evacuated during the war to Blaenau Ffestiniog in Wales (where he later went on his honeymoon). They stayed in Wales for about 3 years while Leslie continued his duties as a fireman in Portsmouth. Luckily Leslie was able to visit regularly. Derek remembers the street parties that took place at the end of the war. He remembers one particular photograph of him and his cousin at a street party.

Derek attended a school approximately two and a half miles from his home. On his way to school he often stopped off at the bakery to buy two buns of hot, fresh bread. These perhaps cost about 1d. (approximately1/2pence) Derek's best friend at school was Brian Putman who has now emmigrated to New Zealand. Derek and Brian keep in contact every now and then via email.

Derek was a well-behaved pupil at school. However he has a distinct memory of making a hole in the pavement with the steel heel on his school shoes. Derek's mum wanted him to attend a private secondary school that her friend's son also attended, she wanted the best for Derek. Derek's favourite subject at school was Maths. He remembers one specific teacher called Mr Caine. Derek and his friends used to say; 'Caine by name, cane by nature.' Derek left school at around age 15. His family didn't own a car; Derek recalls that only very lucky people had a car because they were so expensive. He then went on to do a Marine Engineering Apprenticeship. Derek earned around 6 or 7 shillings a week, (approximately 30 or 40pence) it wasn't a lot but he learnt to get by.

Derek met his wife Janet when he was aged 18. She was on holiday in Portsmouth and he met her at a tennis tournament. Janet lived in Leicester so they stayed in contact by writing letters to one another. After he had completed his apprenticeship at age 21, Derek moved to Leicester where he and Janet, who was then 22, got married in a Methodist Church. They went to Wales on their honeymoon for a week where they stayed in the mountains. Derek also got his first car when he was 21. It was a Rover and cost between £200-£300. Derek enjoyed driving and liked showing his new car off because not many people his age had one.

After his apprenticeship it was compulsory for Derek to do his National Service. Most men went into the Army but Derek didn't want to so he applied for the Royal Navy. Unfortunately he failed his medical test due to a chill in his bladder, this annoyed Derek a lot. He then went on to work for the Merchant Navy for six years, working in an engine room. Derek does not regret this decision as some of the best years of his life were spent travelling at sea. The best place Derek visited was South Africa, he loved it and could easily have lived there. Derek was at sea for 6-9 weeks at a time but was still able to see his wife regularly.

Derek remembers buying his first house in Albion Street, with his wife. Janet was nervous about spending so much money but she agreed to keep working so that they could afford the mortgage. They do not regret the decision. They bought their house from another man named Derek. They paid £3,125 for their house and Derek remembers how great it was when he finally paid it all off.

Janet worked at the Premier Drum factory (the building is still there today next to Tesco) until she had their first child, Belinda. They went on to have two more girls; Suzanne and Alison with a two year gap between them. All of Derek's children live locally in Leicester and he sees them regularly. Belinda and Suzanne both work in schools and Alison works in Debenhams. Some of Derek's fondest memories have been watching his children grow up healthily and happily. Derek now has five grandchildren; Nathan, Ryan, Emma, Hayley and Joanne. Joanne and her husband David have two daughters. So Derek has two great granddaughters Summer and Chelsea.

Five years ago Derek and Janet went to Australia for 3 months where they visited relatives and went to Sydney. This is where Janet first saw the great cruise ships. They now really enjoy going on cruises together, now that their children are all grown up. They have been on the Queen Mary and Queen Elizabeth.

Derek started coming to Age UK Oadby and Wigston sometime during the year 2000. He fondly remembers receiving his 10 year volunteer certificate. Derek started the table tennis coaching at the Centre, as he loves to play. He also enjoys golf and still regularly plays.

In 2004 Derek became a Trustee of the charity and has also helped to raise money for a new mini-bus. He now volunteers as an escort on the bus for the friends who come to the Centre for lunch, helping them into and out of the bus and to home. Volunteers like Derek are the lifeblood of our charity and we are very grateful for all of his work.

KATHLEEN
CARVER

Kath was born on the 17th of August 1925 in Wigston, to Charles Whyatt and his wife. Kath has lived in Wigston all her life. She had one brother and five sisters. In order of their births they were Dorothy, Kath, Margaret, Donald, Nora and Sylvia. Their father was a Director of Johnson and Barnes and they made and sold silk socks and stockings. They were quite a wealthy family and lived in a large house called Belmont House, which is next to where the current Council Offices are now. The family owned the second car in Wigston, which allowed them to travel all over the country on their holidays.

Her brother, Donald went to the Wyggeston Grammar School and as a result, knows the Attenborough's very well. Kathleen went to a national school until she went to South Wigston Intermediate School, until she was 15. This required her passing all of her exams. When she left school Kath worked in the offices of Taylor, Taylor, Hobsons. They made optical lenses.

At the age of 17, in 1942 she joined the Women's Royal Air Force and worked on telecommunications earning about 10 shillings per week. (This is 50p in current money.) Kath was brought up in quite a strict family and she was very shocked when she first joined the WRAF as she was suddenly expected to get undressed and changed in front of the other girls in her quarters. This was very embarrassing for Kath but she soon got used to it. In 1943 she was moved to Germany where she worked at several camps, as she was moved from camp to camp depending on the situation. It wasn't until 1946 she left for home, but in 1947 she went back to Germany working on telecommunications with the Civil Service.

In 1950 she finally came home and was reacquainted with Robert (known as Bob), whom she had met at school. They met again when they both went dancing in Leicester. They married in the early 1950's when Kath was working for the engineering company, Wildt Mellor Bromley. She was able to use her WRAF knowledge as she worked with the telex machine sending messages to customers all over the world. Bob and Kath lived with her parents for a short while, at Belmont House on Station Road in Wigston. Kath's sister, Margaret married Ted Williams.*

Kath was unable to work for long though, as she was soon expecting her first child, Michael and the family moved into their own home. Bob was a mechanic who mended sock machines, and they first lived in a council house where they raised their family. They had one more son, Anthony, and a daughter, Sharon. Michael travels around the world a lot because of his job, but she still gets to see Anthony and Sharon and their children very often. In 2010 Kath had a very serious heart operation. Kath believes that this has affected her memory and she has not been able to remember quite a lot of the details of her life. Eventually Kath moved out of her home and into a flat at William Peardon Court in Wigston. She has made new friends there and enjoys playing bingo with the other residents. Kath's daughter, Sharon lives in Kibworth and she also goes to the Mecca Bingo with Kath and they often enjoy driving out to the shops. Shopping is one of Kath's pleasures and she and Sharon have many drives out in Sharon's car.

Kath met Margaret Moss* whilst living on Station Road and they became very close friends. They visited Age Concern (later Age UK) Oadby and Wigston together for many years. Kath has been a very loyal supporter of the charity, and supplier of chocolate, and still enjoys lunch with her friends every week.

*See chapter on Mary Williams.
*See chapter on Margaret Moss.

BRENDA
COLGATE

Brenda was born on 2nd September in 1945 in Leicester. She and her sister, a year and 26 days younger, Gillian were raised by their mother and grandmother in Leicester.

Brenda's mother, Irene Taylor, worked part time in the canteen at Leicester Royal Infirmary. Brenda does not feel that she ever went without during her childhood and has fond memories of the family holiday to Skegness every summer. The family would go for a week, travelling up on the train having sent the luggage up in advance.
Brenda failed her 11 plus exam and attended Sir Jonathan North Secondary School - an all girls school where she remembers Miss McCarthy.

Brenda thought positively of her school and particularly enjoyed sports, her reason being that "it wasn't such hard work!" The school was quite strict, especially regarding cleanliness. The headmistress, for example, used to be particularly strict towards litter louts. Away from school Brenda would spend time playing with her friends, particularly Tina who lived on the same street. Common activities included hopscotch and skipping.

Brenda left school at the age of 15 and went to work in Woolworths in Leicester city centre. At the age of 17, in 1962 she joined the army as a cook, working in the Woman's Royal Army Corp. in Aldershot and then in the border of Sussex/Essex. She worked as a cook for the ordinary officers mess but also had the chance to do some 'posh cooking' in the private officer's dining room. During this time Brenda met David George Colgate in a pub in Sussex.

They were married at the registry office in Redhill, Surrey, on 11th July in 1964. Brenda wore a blue costume and hat. Brenda left the army and the new family lived in rented accommodation in Sussex.

They lived in Sussex for about a year and then moved to Leicester to live with Brenda's family.

On 5th May 1965 Kevin Edward was born and on 18th January 1967 Andrew was born. They were living with Brenda's Grandma until they were able to move into a council house on The Fairway where they stayed for eighteen years. In 1997 they moved to a house in Wigston but it was hard work to be able to pay for it and Brenda had three jobs to make ends meet.

Kevin married and moved to Birmingham where he died of kidney failure aged 47.

Brenda mostly took cleaning jobs as it fitted in with the family schedule and avoided the need for babysitters. Kevin and Brenda divorced in 1984. Brenda shares the belief that families were more disciplined in the past than they are in the modern day. She also believes there was more of a community feel. She recalls that there would be two toilets to be shared among six houses. Although times may have been harder, they were 'happier', Brenda says.

Leicester, according to Brenda, has changed dramatically over time but not for the better. The best buildings have been replaced and there are too many shops now. The price of goods is another noticeable change, with things becoming more expensive following the introduction of the decimal system in the 1970s. Brenda also believes that the modern day is too internet based and admits she struggles with the use of her mobile phone and cannot use a computer. The influx of cars is another dramatic change. Brenda remembers how the buses were more efficient in the past and also how people tried to avoid the bus conductor in order to get on the buses for free. Brenda's grandmother used to have to wake her up in the mornings (Brenda admits that she was not a morning person) in order to prevent her from missing the bus for work.

When Brenda's sons grew up and left home she began to work in a care home for elderly people. She enjoyed her work and left only when it was time to retire in 2005. Before retiring Brenda volunteered at Age Concern Oadby and Wigston but when it was necessary to work on Saturdays she had to give up her voluntary work. After her retirement Brenda returned to her voluntary work at Age UK Oadby and Wigston. She now volunteers with Douglas, who she met in a pub about five years ago and they have been friends for a social life full of concerts, films and weekends away. Brenda has been a most valuable supporter of Age UK Oadby and Wigston ever since as she is "always at the end of the phone". Thank you Brenda.

BARRY
DODGE

Barry was born in Leicester in a nursing home in 1935 to Albert Dodge and Evelyn (nee Joyce). He also has two sisters, Joyce, named after his mother's family, who is 6 years older than him and Beryl who is 18 months younger. Barry's Dad had his own business selling hairdressing supplies. Albert and Evelyn divorced after an affair he had with his secretary when Barry was just 10 years old.

Barry was very upset by the divorce. To make matters worse, people at school gave Barry a hard time and gossiped about it as it was something frowned upon by society. Particularly as his father had gone off with another woman, there was not much sympathy. Barry says it is something he has never really got over.

Life got quite complicated for Barry and he went to live with his aunt in Coventry after the divorce, at the age of 12. It was during the war, when Coventry experienced very bad bombings. Barry remembers seeing barrage balloons over Coventry. He and his family often used the air raid shelters. The family had an air raid shelter of their own in the garden but as it often flooded it wasn't very useful. The communal shelter was in the local laundry and they often went there with their neighbours. Barry remembers lots of singing and trying to make the most of the time. To get away from the bombings Barry moved back to Leicester and lived with his Mum in Humberstone and attended Mundella School.

School was something Barry has said he never really enjoyed. Due to moving between Coventry and Leicester he found it difficult to settle and make friends. He was also a bit of a trouble maker. He was punished for bunking off school and playing in clay pits in Barkby, a village in north-east Leicester; an area that suffered bombing and was hence very dangerous. On one occasion, a neighbour of Barry's reported him to the police for truancy but luckily for him, he was too young to be punished and got away with a slap on the wrist!

Whilst Barry was at school aged 14 he met a girl called Glydneth (a Welsh name). They were "very, very good friends". After leaving school they enjoyed going dancing which they were able to do 3 or 4 times per week. They went to The Palais, The Bell Hotel, which was on the corner of Charles Street and Humberstone Gate, the Trocadero on Uppingham Road and even the Fire Station on Lancaster Road. When Glyn left school she worked making paper carrier bags and then went on to making optical lenses. Barry left school at 15 years old and went to work with his father in the warehouse at 10 Churchgate in Leicester, this is now Brucciani's, Barry helped with the accounts. Barry found it difficult because his father had two families to support and when life became too difficult and he was ready to leave, his best friend offered him a job with the accounts department for his sign company on Oakland Road in Leicester. The job was very enjoyable as it was a family business. Barry remained there for 25 years and retired aged 65.

Barry and Glyn were married in 1958 at St Peter's Church in Highfields, Leicester. Glyn's family lived on Melbourne Road and this was their local church. Barry and Glyn moved to Wigston when they married and lived in Duffield Avenue for a few years. Glyn was diagnosed with TB and was advised to not get pregnant. Barry and Glyn decided to take the risk and they succeeded and a son, Carlton was born at the City General Hospital in 1960. They then decided that the risk to Glyn's health was too great and he remained their only child. A short while later the houses on the other side of Welford Road were being built and the family moved to Brighton Avenue. Barry remembers family holidays in Torquay then Majorca and the Spanish mainland. The weather and temperature were good for Glyn's health so they enjoyed their holidays abroad.

Carlton attended schools in Wigston – Bell Street, where Sainsbury's is now, Waterleys, Abington and Guthlaxton. Barry remembers that whilst Carlton was a student he got a holiday job on a construction site and it was the demolition of his old school and the building of Sainsbury's. Carlton attended the University of Reading to read physics. He gained a doctorate and then went on to work in research. He worked for the De Beers diamond company. He married Elizabeth (Libby) and they lived in Didcot. They moved to the Isle of Man where Carlton continued with to work in research. He has also worked with a government nuclear establishment.

Barry has three grandchildren; James born in 1986, Michael born in 1988 and Sara Jayne born in 1994. James gained a degree in English Literature and now works as a proof reader for a magazine. He met his partner, Holly at school. Michael studied engineering at the University of Leicester and that is how he met his partner, Amber. Michael has now completed a PhD at Cambrige Univeristy. Sara Jayne is studying law at University in Chester.

In 2006/7 Glyn was diagnosed with cancer and Barry was able to nurse her until she went in to hospital. Sadly she died in 2008. Since then Barry has lived on his own and believes that he has been "pretty good" at looking after himself. Recently he has been more immobile and has moved to living on the ground floor of the house. This has been quite disruptive and Barry has taken a while to get used to it. At this point in our chat Barry remembered that he had recently had a bit of an 'adventure' when he 'lost' his wallet. Having used his wallet he decided to hide it before going out. When he returned he couldn't remember where he'd hidden it. Thinking that he had lost it he cancelled all of his cards and informed his bank and then found the wallet under a cushion on the settee. (Luckily we all have weird moments so can sympathise with him.)

Barry's sister and his friends now help him to cope with living on his own. His friend, Bridget helps with the groceries and housework and he really appreciates her help. Barry is a very calm and gentle man and is very happy enjoying his lunch on the 'men's table' at Age UK Oadby and Wigston every week from Monday to Thursday. On Friday he meets his sisters. Joyce's husband, Stan died some years ago and she now lives alone on Jean Drive. However she has 15 great grandchildren so has a busy time at Christmas. She arranges for a taxi to collect her to bring her to Wigston for lunch with Barry and Beryl. Beryl, who has two daughters, lives in Markfield and sometimes the sisters can travel together.

To Celebrate the Life of

Barry Dodge

13th February 1935 - 18th September 2016

Gilroes Crematorium

Friday 30th September 2016

at 1.00 pm

FLORENCE
DRAGE

Florence was born at home on 2nd March 1928 in Durkar, near Wakefield. It was a very foggy night and Florence's father had to go to fetch the doctor. It was so hard to see anything that her Dad walked past his own home twice before he could find his way. Florence's Dad was Frederick Clement Pettit; a chauffeur to the Managing Director of the Barnsley Brewery who lived at Durkar House. Florence's Mum was Francis Annie nee Dickinson.

Florence had a brother called Charles Edward. He was twelve years older than Florence and was a pupil at Wakefield Grammar School when Florence was born. Charles left school and became an accountant. When war broke out he became a pilot and flew Spitfires. It is believed that on a bright sunny day the German bombers had been to Liverpool and on their way home they flew over Wales. Charles was in the air to intercept them but they came out of the sunlight towards his Spitfire and he was killed. Charles is buried in the graveyard in Olney because the family thought that he should be close to home.

The family had moved to Olney, in Buckinghamshire, in 1932. Olney is a very prestigious town. There is a lace museum and the Cowper and Newton Museum; the writers of poems and hymns including 'Amazing Grace'. More important than these, in Florence's memories, is the annual Pancake Race. This event is reputed to have been run since 1445. It was revived after a break in 1948. A book written by Graham Lenton based upon the memories of his mother called 'The story of The Olney Pancake Race' features a photograph of some of the competitors in the race with Florence's mother, Frances Pettit in the right of the photograph. In 1950 Liberal, a small town in Kansas, USA issued an international challenge and the two towns have competed against each other since. One photograph which Florence has shows that the American Embassy supported the race by presenting the prize to the winner. The race is won in both towns but the best time is recorded for the final winner. Florence took part in the race on one occasion and photograph of her in the 1949 race appears in the book, she came second that year. She has also kept her certificate showing that she took part in the race.

One competitor was 80 years old, Mrs Gladys Dillingham who 'walked' the race 23 times. 'The Standard' newspaper of 1986 shows that 21 competitors took part. It has obviously been a big part of the lives of many residents of Olney – not only for Florence. Having attended the Pancake Race in 2016 Florence is planning to donate her cuttings and publications to the Race Committee. Apparently the American town of Liberal have a museum dedicated to the Race so her documents could be the start of something very important.

During those years in Olney Florence was very much involved in local life. She has kept a large number of photographs and mementoes of these activities. Florence also says that she remembers that Olney was a town because it had a cattle market. Olney is where Florence first went to school. She found it difficult to settle in to school because she had a very broad Yorkshire accent, so no-one could understand her. She remembers standing next to the piano crying because she was so unhappy. The teacher that Florence remembers as being kind was Miss Smith. Florence had good friends from school, two of them were called Mary and Dorothy.

They met when they first started school so have been friends since the age of four. They were in the Brownies, Girl Guides, Sea Rangers and St John's Ambulance Cadets together. Florence and Dorothy went through junior school together until they took the 11 plus exam. Florence passed the exam and attended Wolverton Grammar School, in the area which was to become Milton Keynes, although it was very different then. Florence and her Mum were members of the church choir. As members of the 'Girls' Friendly Society' they put on plays and one of Florence's memories is of singing 'Three Sisters' with Dorothy. The friendship didn't end because they were at different schools and in fact Dorothy was godmother to Florence's son, Brian.

Getting to her new school was quite difficult for Florence as she had to go by bus and then by train to Wolverton. Eventually they asked the local Education Authority why they couldn't travel all the way by bus and this is what did happen so that made it easier, a matter of pride for Florence that a young man called Gordon did most of the campaigning!

Florence met her future husband, Gordon whilst she was still at school, as he was a friend of her next door neighbour. The two boys enjoyed shooting and were able to work around the local farms shooting pheasants. Florence is sure that this was quite legal.

Just as we record this interview Florence and her family have renovated and sold her mother-in-law's cottage in Olney. That is the last link to the area. A sad parting.

Florence left school at age 16 and went to work in the local tax office. This was a very responsible job and she had to appear in court when prosecuting tax cheats. She remembers that one time the defendant was very angry and was shouting at Florence but luckily there was a witness so she was rescued. One of the things that Florence remembers about this time is that she paid 1/6d for a return ticket to work. This is approximately 12pence. Florence remembers that there was a hockey team at the Tax Office and she played many games in Northampton. Florence worked at the tax office for 5 years, until she was twenty one. Gordon was a trainee surveyor in Newport Pagnall. In 1949 when he qualified he was employed by Wigston Council so they moved to Leicestershire and lived in one of the local council houses. They lived in council houses for 12 years, then Gordon eventually realised his dream of building his own family home after many years of searching for the ideal plot of land.

Florence had transferred to the tax office in Leicester and both Florence and Gordon played for the hockey team there. The team was called 'Lillie House' Gordon really enjoyed his job and one of the highlights that Florence remembers is him being interviewed and photographed for the local newspaper. He was quoted as saying that all of the problems in Wigston could be solved with a bypass. Florence thinks it's amusing that Wigston still hasn't got a bypass!
In 1953 Florence and Gordon had a son, Brian, and three years later a daughter, Patricia was born. Florence made many of her clothes and ballet dresses. This clearly set a good example to Tricia as she is now an expert needlewoman.

In 1965 Florence applied for a pre-college course which led to qualifications as a teacher. She attended the Scraptoft campus and this involved quite bit of travel. At this time another of the students was Avis Ambler* and she lived close to Florence so they shared the cars to college for three years until they left in 1968. Both of them then worked at Waterleys Primary School in Wigston and Avis became a very important friend. Gordon stayed at Wigston Council until he became ill in 1976. He underwent an operation for blood clots but it wasn't successful. As a result of this Gordon suffered a stroke and wasn't able to work any longer. He was only 50 years old.

*See chapter on Avis Ambler.

Florence worked really hard to keep Gordon at home and allow her to look after him herself. She had to keep working to look after Gordon although he was able to attend a stroke club and Day Centre. This gave him the opportunity to begin to paint with his left hand. He had always been keen to draw but now had to learn to work with his 'other' hand. Florence speaks lovingly of the pictures which she still has that Gordon was able to produce during this time. Florence moved to work at Thurnby Primary School. This helped to provide the money needed to continue to care for Gordon at home. This was a very happy time for Florence and she really enjoyed her job. In the 1980's Florence moved to Merrydale Primary School as Deputy Head and experienced quite a culture shock. Having become used to the lovely countryside outside of the school in a very rural setting she now worked in a city school with a distinct lack of cows to watch. The Head Teacher had a heart attack and was unable to continue working for a short time so Florence was promoted to Head Teacher to cover the absence. Florence retired from Merrydale when she was 60 years old. However, this didn't last long and she was asked to return to cover an absent colleague. She retired again and yet again went back to help out. Eventually Florence retired aged 63 and although she therefore retired three times she is keen to point out that she didn't receive three leaving presents! Florence remembers that when she retired she was told that "If anyone asks you out – go." She has really taken this advice to heart and tries to fit everything in to a busy life. Her family have expanded and they are very important to her and she loves spending time with them.

Brian has worked with various UK water companies for 30 years and now runs his own Consultancy business advising on drinking water treatment projects. Brian is married to Paula and they have two sons, Andrew and John. Both are very tall young men and Florence jokes that she has to ask permission to kiss them as she can't reach, so they have to bend down. Andrew is a bank manager in Bristol. Brian and Paula now live in Burton-upon-Trent to be near John and his family. John is a Director of a sports company, and his wife, Deb is a Head of Science in a Secondary School. They have a daughter called Anna.

Florence is thoroughly enjoying being a Great Grandma. Some of her time is now spent volunteering in the shop for Age UK Oadby and Wigston. This is very tempting for Florence and Anna seems to 'need' lots of presents. Tricia lives with her partner Phil and works as a professional seamstress. Tricia has a daughter called Remy Susanah. It seems that only her grandma calls her by both names. Grandma's can get away with that though! Remy studied a degree in history at Northampton University. She now teaches Dance.

Away from her family Florence has been a member of Inner Wheel in Wigston. Florence was President in 1988 and she organised a charity football match. Oadby Town against a team from Leicester City Football Club. The generous funds were donated to the Stroke Club. Sadly, after existing for 38 years, this organisation has had to close as members have reduced in number.

As Florence has been the treasurer for the last twelve years she has recently been shredding piles of documents. The members have now joined the Oadby Inner Wheel so the commitment continues. Another of the "If you are asked" activities was working with the Red Cross. Her long time friend Avis and Florence spent hours working in a care home in South Wigston helping to do shopping and they became very proficient at manicures painting other people's fingernails. They also joined a Professional Women's Club. This is now an arts group and Florence enjoys a wide variety of activities. She has always enjoyed getting out and about and remembers taking Gordon to lots of places whilst she could still manage to drive him around. Unfortunately Gordon had a bad fall in the dining room at home and needed to go to hospital. It was decided that having looked

after him for 24 years Florence was not able to continue to keep him at home as his needs increased. Reluctantly Gordon was able to live in a care home but his health continued to deteriorate and he died shortly after, aged 76.

Florence was one of the founding members of U3A in Countesthorpe during 1976/77 and still attends many of their meetings. Another activity which Florence has enjoyed since her retirement is swimming. She is a member of the 'Over 55's Swimming Group' and they are a group of people who have become very good friends. Whilst Gordon was able to travel they often went on holiday with some of these friends and Florence is grateful for the support that they gave to her and Gordon.

Andrew, John, Philip, Paula, Florence, Brian, Tricia, Lucy, Remy Sue, Debbie

Being a member of this group has enabled Florence to travel around the world. They have about 30 members who meet to swim, socialise and plan their trips, locally and internationally. They have annual events which are very special. They go to Thursford in Norfolk for a Christmas Concert and meal. The music ranges from military bands and organ music and including a variety of choirs. Turkey and Tinsel Nights are another annual feature and include the families of the members. Christmas has always been a special time for Florence and her family. In 1939, when her father was made redundant from his job as a chauffeur, when his employer died, Florence spent some time living with her Grandmother in Grantham.

Little did Florence realise that she was attending Kesteven Grantham Girls' School with Margaret Roberts, better known as Margaret Thatcher. A very clear memory is of having Christmas with her Grandmother in Grantham and then going home to Olney to have a second Christmas with her brother who was on leave for the holiday. This was his last Christmas so has very special memories. She also has happy memories of playing games with her Dad and he always loved taking part. This wasn't the only time that Florence managed to celebrate Christmas twice as, when she was a teacher, she would have Christmas at school with the children and then again the big celebration at home with her family. Clever lady! Florence now enjoys spending time with her much larger family and they really look after her over the holiday.

When Florence lived with her parents her mother took her to the theatre in Northampton and this has remained a passion for her. Frequent trips to the Little Theatre in Leicester are organised by Florence for her wide range of friends. In the past she went to the Haymarket Theatre and has been to Curve but she has remained loyal to the Little Theatre for many years.

Florence has volunteered for Age Concern Oadby and Wigston for many years. She has served as a Trustee of the charity and helped with the development of the newly named Age UK Oadby and Wigston. She has worked in the coffee shop and lately in the shop. It has been a very important aspect of her life and she has been a very valuable supporter of the charity. We are very grateful for her efforts and enthusiasm. At this stage Florence became concerned about the amount of time which our interview was taking but I hope that you have read with pleasure the reminiscences of this enthusiastic and gregarious woman. Remember - "If you are asked out – go"!

DOREEN
EAMES

Doreen was born on the 1st August 1926 in Southport, Lancashire. She was an only child and had few aunties and uncles. She felt she had a lonely childhood because of this.

Until she was married, she worked as an accountant and an assisting cashier in Woolworth's. In her earlier days, she described herself as very active and healthy and loved to cook.

As a teenager, Doreen loved dancing and went out all the time. This is where she met her husband Derek. When Doreen first told her mother about her new boyfriend, she said "I've heard that too many times" and Doreen replied with "no, this is real this time". Doreen and Derek were married for 58 years before he passed away.

They both retired at 65 and moved to Spain straight after, where they lived for 14 years. They had great times meeting 'lovely people' and being 'very happy together'. They lived in a villa with a swimming pool and a beautiful view, where they very quickly made friends with the locals.

In Spain, they made 2 very good friends Carol and Jeffery. In Doreen's words, they were 'the best of friends' and would spend Christmas's and New Year's together like one family.

Derek passed away in Spain a few years ago. Soon after this, Doreen moved back to Leicester to be with her 2 sons and grandchildren.

She has been coming to Age UK Oadby and Wigston for her lunch for many years now.

MARGARET (PEGGY)
EVANS

Peggy was born in Manchester in 1931. She had an older sister, Catherine (Kitty) Mary Tudor Evans. Both were brought up by their Mother, Morfydd (better known as Della) , when her marriage ended. Peggy never knew any other way of life so living with Mother in one house and visiting Father in another was just a way of life. "It was in the agreement" so that was that.

As a former teacher Della taught both Kitty and Peggy to read before they went to school and, as they grew older, taught them to play the piano and there was plenty of singing – well, she was Welsh!

There were financial difficulties when the 'agreed' living allowance didn't materialise but Della supplemented funds by entertaining (songs at the piano) at various private functions. This developed into more variety work as a pianist/

DEANSGATE, MANCHESTER.

Image Source: http://www.oldstratforduponavon.com/manchester2.html

accompanist and concert parties to straight acting at the Theatre Royal in Horsefair Street, Leicester. Both Kitty and Peggy had this mixed background of academia and 'show biz'.

The family came to Leicester in 1937. Peggy went to Bell Street Junior School and was still there when war broke out. Peggy remembers how they sheltered under the stairs like frightened rabbits with Mummy Rabbit putting on an air of calm during the first air-raid warning. No bombs fell before the all clear sounded so it didn't take many false alarms before they carried on living as normal. They adapted to rationing – even sweets. Kitty organised a 'Children Only Garden Party' in aid of the Spitfire Fund. Peggy's allocated role was telling fortunes with playing cards at 1/2d at a time. (This is such a small amount that there is no comparison amount in today's money.) They raised the princely sum of 5shillings (25p) but captured the imagination as they had a mention on the wireless (radio).

Della had moved on from variety and was acting at the Theatre Royal in Horsefair Street in Leicester (now a bank). Kitty was also acting occasionally as well but it wasn't until she was 12 that Peggy had her licence to perform in a professional theatre. She played Adele in 'Jane Eyre' and can proudly claim that her first leading man (playing Rochester) was Donald Sinden. Later on that year the Education Department was appealing for married women to go back to teaching

Image: https://uk.pinterest.com/pin/86412886578764309/

and Della opted for a less precarious existence with a regular, reliable income and started teaching in Bell Street Infants School. In October of that year there was a final 'swan song' when, according to the programme " Miss Peggy Evans, Ballerina, accompanied by Miss Della Hague" (Morfydd's stage name) appeared in the cabaret at a Thé Dansant in aid of The Duke of Gloucester's Red Cross and St. John's Fund held in Claridges, London. They stayed in Grosvenor House, Park Lane, with Morfydd's sister, Mrs E Bowen Davis (Auntie Katy to Peggy) who had arranged it all. She was Vice Chairman of the organising committee. So Peggy and her Mum enjoyed a weekend savouring the delights of 'high society'.

Both Kitty and Peggy were in Kibworth Grammar School by then and were there when the war ended. Both of them joined in the celebrations in Bell Street and were singing and dancing round the Bank until the early hours of the morning. Peggy really loved being in Kibworth. Many friends from Long Street School went on the school bus every day and she made new friends there as well. She tended to enjoy the maths and science subjects most and there was also the lighter side of school plays and music festivals to join in. Peggy stayed on to do the Higher School Certificate (A levels), by which time Kitty had finished her studies at Goldsmiths College and was teaching in Bell Street!

Peggy left school at 18 to go to the University College of Wales in Aberystwyth, where she studied Botany, Zoology and Chemistry. She learnt a lot and played a bit more – Bridge School excelled – she wrote material and performed in Rag Week variety concerts, took part in the Debates Union; singing and after two glorious years ended up with half a degree and a job in the soil research department of the Welsh Plant Breeding Station. She enjoyed the variety of the work but after two years came back to Leicester.

However, just before she left the University she had a lovely time going to Kitty's wedding in London. Kitty had already left Wigston and was teaching in London where she met Peter. It was a whirlwind romance and it worked.

Meanwhile back in Leicester Peggy started work at BB Chemical Co. Ltd. (the old name for Bostik) She took to the private sector like a duck to water. The general atmosphere was less formal – colleagues became life-long friends.

She started as a lab assistant and worked her way up. The company had a social life of it's own and the initial works outing to London wetted her appetite for more regular day trips which she would go on with friends. This stood her in good stead when, as a chemical buyer, she had to make her own way down to various chemical exhibitions in Earl's Court.

Image: http://www.gracesguide.co.uk/File:Im19440810FL-Bostik.jpg

Peggy also joined the Drama Society – naturally – and entertained at the Christmas parties in the canteen for the employees children and also the pensioners who'd left the company. Kitty had four children by now and the impromptu sing-a-longs that took place when Nana played the piano for the children were good practise for these Christmas parties.

After 14 years Peggy began to feel there must be a world outside and left Bostik and took a 12 month sabbatical. She only took temporary, part-time jobs. She dabbled in writing humerous articles for magazines but never sold enough to live on. Her two favourite jobs were market research on the trains and taking bets with the Tote at various race meetings up and down the country. Both supplied living expenses and gave plenty of time between each individual job to look around the towns and cities of England – like a working holiday. In between all of this she took part time clerical/secretarial jobs through an employment agency.

It was at the last one of these, at Dunlop, that she was offered the job of office manager in their plastics department. Peggy liked Dunlop but there was a more 'corporate atmosphere' than the 'old family business' – it was quite noticeable. The job was mostly production planning and customer liaison. Her London visits came in handy when she went with her boss to the Plastics Exhibition and she was able to guide him via the shortest route to Earl's Court. Peggy was settling in nicely when the entire department was transferred to Wrexham. This was too far from London for Peggy and it just happened that Dunlop had started a new department – the Electrical Products Group and she became office manager there. Same title but an entirely different job! Now she was responsible for preparing bids for the supply of components for power lines and, if they were successful, processing the order papers.

During her time at Bostik Peggy had completed two Leicester University Certificate courses, one in Sociology and one in Industrial Administration. Now she went one better and did a part-time degree course with the Open University in Maths and Technology and finally got her BA. A couple of years later her new boss emigrated to Canada and Peggy finally reached the heady heights of senior management when she became Contracts Manager. Two years later they were taken over by Brush Power but stayed in Leicester. Peggy got on well with the new management and was nice and settled when another two years later the whole lot was taken over by Hawker Siddley and everything was transferred to Banbury – and they say show business is a precarious existence!

This time Peggy took the generous redundancy money and had a very leisurely sabbatical. She joined a playwrights group in Knighton and started writing topical comedy material for BBC Radio and had a modest success writing for 'The News Huddlines' and 'Weekending'. This developed into a hobby for many years to come, until both were axed in a big radio shake-up. She was also able to go on more holidays with the local natural history group at Vaughan College. Her mother had been retired a long time and was still very active so they were able to spend more time together and nip down to see Kitty for the day in Stevenage. The children had all flown the nest by now but Kitty was still teaching.

They celebrated Della's 80th birthday together in Leicester (she didn't want too much fuss). Consequently it came as a big shock 5 months later when Kitty died suddenly. Peggy feels that her mother never really recovered from it but she did gradually return to her old ways and her friends at the bridge club were very supportive. Peggy's writing group finished and she joined the Phoenix Writers group and actually sold some material to television. She had also started as a volunteer helper in Adult Basic Education teaching adult literacy and numeracy. This eventually led to paid work teaching her own classes and a half time permanent post with more responsibilities, this fitted in well with her variety script department efforts for the BBC tv.

Image: http://www.bbc.co.uk/historyofthebbc/buildings/lime-grove

Peggy went to a variety script writers meeting in Lime Grove Studios and met masses of other part-timers who were battling for a bit of air space. The meeting was to launch 'Three of a Kind' with Lenny Henry, Tracey Ullman and David Copperfield (comedian, not magician). They turned up and Lenny Henry chatted to Peggy – but she did stick out like a sore thumb as the only other woman in the room! When the programme finally came out Peggy had won all of 20 seconds of air-space on the programme that won the Silver Rose at the International Montreux Festival. She did sell a few other bits but stuck to the day job. Peggy retired from all responsibilities when she was 60 but did keep on with her "Maths for the Terrified" classes until she was 63 when – after three mini-strokes her mother's short-term memory loss was becoming severe.

Peggy's mother died in 1999 and Peggy returned to the land of the living, birdwatching and natural history weekends plus day trips and holidays with Woods Coaches.

Nowadays Peggy has given up all those healthy outdoor pursuits and prefers the warmth of cities with cafes and art galleries and museums.

Peggy moved to Beech Court in 2010 as the house and garden were getting 'bigger' or more hard work. She also wanted to make the move while she was still young enough to adapt to the change. She shares her time between Beech Court, Age UK Oadby and Wigston and the Richard Attenborough Art Centre, where she does classes in art and 'Singing for Fun' choral singing. Then day trips with Woods Coaches mainly to Liverpool, London and Oxford but if the coaches are going to Leeds, Cambridge or Bath then she goes to visit her nieces and nephew.

Peggy feels very lucky that she is still able to get out and about and has the experience to confidently "do her own thing" when she wants to. Looking back, doing this interview has made her realise that "life's been good – warts and all!"

SYLVIA MAY
GASK

Sylvia was born to Thomas Henry and Elizabeth Anne Hall on 20th August 1932 at home, in the kitchen!

Elizabeth also gave birth to Sylvia's younger siblings, Bernard; Albert; Brian; Graham and Terry. To help to support her family Elizabeth was able to do the washing and ironing for five school masters as well as cleaning at the local pub in Markfield, The Bull's Head. (How did she find the time?) She died aged 35.

The family lived in a 2 bedroomed terraced house in Markfield. Sylvia slept in the kitchen as she was the only girl, so couldn't share the bedroom with her brothers. The house had no bathroom so a tin bath was kept in the scullery and everyone bathed in the kitchen. Sylvia hated being watched by her brothers when she was in the bath so tried to avoid being seen.

Sylvia attended Primary School in Markfield and later went to South Charnwood School. Aged 10 years old Sylvia was diagnosed with cancer and was treated by Mr Ireland at the Leicester Royal Infirmary. She remembers him as a man with jet black hair. Being away from home for the first time was frightening for her and the operation to remove her womb was to be a lasting memory for the young child.

Sylvia left school at 16 and worked in a shoe factory in Anstey. She also spent some time in a printing company and then returned to a shoe factory, in Leicester. It was at her first workplace that Sylvia met a man nine years older than her called Henry Charles Gask. Everyone called him Harry. The romance was to lead to their marriage at the Leicester Registry Office. Sylvia wore a blue suit and she thinks that her bouquet might have contained carnations. The newly married couple lived in their own home in New Parks, followed by a move to a house in Hawthorne Street in the Newfoundpool area of Leicester. This time they had two bedrooms and a bathroom.

Harry and Sylvia were unable to have children and adopted a daughter, Julie when she was 6 weeks old.

When Julie was a child the family visited her Uncle Terry who lived in Taunton. It was a good place for holidays. He and his wife have a boy and girl with similar ages to Julie. The family also enjoyed holidays to Bridlington, Whitby and Great Yarmouth so have covered the north and south of England.

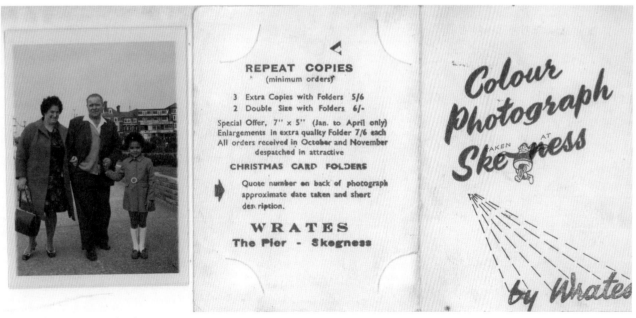

Sylvia, Harry and Julie

They enjoyed many foreign holidays to Malta, Yugoslavia and other European countries. Harry died in 1991 and Sylvia continued to go on holiday on her own.

Julie is now married and lives in Knighton. She works as a Field Care Supervisor for a private care company.

Harry and Sylvia

JOYCE
HALLS

Joyce was born to John Raymond Simpson and Edith Marion Blamire in 1930 in Leicester. John was a fireman on the railways in Suffolk where he lived until meeting Edith, a tailoress. Joyce had an older brother, Alan Desmond who was born in 1927 and a younger brother, William born in 1933.

One of her earliest memories is of going to a nursery for the first time. Her Mum left her for the morning and Joyce remembers that the children were to lie on straw mats for a nap but all Joyce could do was cry, as she didn't like her Mum leaving her there on her own.

Joyce attended St George's Primary School on St George's Street in Leicester, and was at this school when they held a party for the coronation of King George after the abdication of his brother Edward.

In 1939 Joyce was living with her family over a fish and chip shop on Humberstone Road when war broke out. Her father was out on duty as an ARP Warden and a dreadful memory for Joyce was that her Mum was getting ready for opening the shop on Friday lunchtime and had got the pans hot ready for cooking the first lot of chips. She put some cold, wet chips into the hot fat and the fat exploded over her Mum who put her arms up to protect her face so her arms and neck got very badly burned. She was wearing a thick cardigan at the time which helped to save her arms from further really bad injuries.

Joyce also remembers the night when Leicester was bombed during the 1939/45 war. The family were supposed to go down to a bomb shelter but her Dad was "having none of it." He walked them all the way to some open fields, which are now the New Parks Estate, and they spent the night under some trees. They watched as the searchlights were tracking the enemy planes and the tracer bullets trying to shoot them down.

Back (l to r)
Joyce Wright, Pat Vines, Betty Small.
Middle (l to r)
Joyce Simpson (me) Irene Musson, Jeanne Protheroe, Phyll Payne.
Front (l to r)
Doreen Webster, Norma Schreder, Edna Schreder, June Wallis, Phyllis Marston.

The family then moved to Hawthorne Street where Joyce went to Ingle Street School. It was here that she met her lifelong friend, Margaret Foley. They both left school when they were eleven and went to King Richard III Intermediate School and both left at the age of 14 to start work in the hosiery trade. Joyce went to work at Wolsey on Abbey Lane and was working in the training centre when the Queen Mother and King George visited Leicester. They came to the training centre and the Queen Mother stood behind Joyce watching her sewing and asked Joyce if she was "enjoying her work?" Joyce replied "Yes, thank you ." as she didn't know what else to say.

Aged 15 and living in Hawthorne Street she met her boyfriend William Halls, who lived over the road. William served his two years in the army in the R.A.M.C. as a hygiene inspector. They were married in August 1953. Joyce was 22 and William was 23. They had two daughters; Lynda born in 1959 and Christine born in 1963.

The family moved to Aylestone in 1964 where they lived for forty years. Whilst the children were growing up Joyce did a number of jobs but mainly worked as a machinist doing 'outdoor' work (working at home on the machines) for the hosiery trade. At one time she was a taxi driver so that she could fit in with the girls' school times.

William joined the St. John Ambulance and over the years rose to the position of Staff Officer. Both daughters also joined the St. John's Ambulance and both William and Lynda won cups for their services. William also served for six years as an escort on the mini-bus for Age Concern in Leicester.

Lynda and Christine grew up and married and had children of their own. Lynda married Michael in 1976 and has a son called Ian who was born in 1977. In 1988 he moved to Redditch. Christine married Roger in 1991 and has three children; Rosie born in 1991, Hannah born in 1993 and Samuel born in 1997.

Joyce and William lived on their own for many years but Joyce was suffering from deteriorating health so, in 2004 they moved to a bungalow close to their daughter Christine in Oadby. Sadly in 2008 William was very poorly and passed away aged 79, just five days after their 55th wedding anniversary.

Joyce now lives on her own but Christine keeps a very good eye on her and makes sure that she has everything that she needs, including lots of shopping trips out and about around Leicestershire.

Joyce has been attending the lunch club at St. Peter's Church Hall for many years and now gets picked up on Mondays by the Age UK Oadby and Wigston mini-bus and travels to Wigston to meet up with friends for lunch. She "has a very tasty three course meal and a good old chat and a laugh." Thanks for your cheerful manner and all of your corny and sometimes cheeky jokes Joyce.

Brother William (Bill) and Joyce

HARRATT

On 18th January 1938 a girl was born to Harold Vincent Langham and his wife Nora, nee Murren, they named their daughter Moya. Harold was a brick maker by trade and in 1940 he joined the Army. On his return he went back to his bricks until he left to become a school caretaker. In 1946 Moya had a brother called Kevin Barry. The family lived on Eastbourne Road in Humberstone.

Moya attended Overton Road Primary School and then their Junior School. Aged 11 Moya moved to Mundella Girls' School. She has fond memories of this school and remembers that she thought that it was a "brilliant school". She particularly liked netball and an unlikely result in a maths test when she came top. Her excuse is that she was the only person to remember to calculate 'time and a half' for

the wages in one of the questions. Another outstanding memory is of a school trip to Derbyshire with her friends, Pamela Berry, Sheila Tookey, Rita Langham and Glenys Jones.

Moya left school aged 15 and went to work at Chilprufe where she was trained to work on the 'Dubied' machine. This was very specialist work making the body section of jumpers and Moya was paid a very good weekly wage of £5 10shillings (£5.50p). As she became more experienced she was promoted to run up to five machines and was paid £25 per week to produce sample garments and fashion jumpers.

During her time at Mundella Moya had enjoyed dancing lessons, especially when they joined the boys from the local school. When she left school Moya began to teach dancing to young children aged 5-8 years. The children were sometimes better than Moya and would point out if she mixed up the steps. Moya covered herself by claiming that she was testing them! Moya attended dance classes herself as an adult and went to the Trocadero on Uppingham Road (now a petrol station) where she often danced with the 'spare' men who didn't have a partner.

Moya was aged 18 when she met Jack and they were married on 6th August 1960 at All Saints Church in Leicester. Moya wore a short white dress which was covered in pearls. Her workmate, Jean was a bridesmaid along with Jack's sister, Marilyn. They both wore lilac dresses.

Jack was working as builder with his Dad, earning about £6 per week. They were building houses in Wigston, which Jack's Dad thought were "a good buy" so the new family bought their first house on Cumberland Road, Wigston Magna

Moya had saved the money for the deposit from her generous wages. She remembers that they had to pay a deposit of £90 when they agreed to buy the house and then as the building progressed they had to pay the next instalments of £90 each time. They eventually obtained a mortgage (£10.9shillings - £10.45p - per month) for the rest of the cost of the house which Moya remembers as being £1,850. An addition to this story is that Jack and Moya originally asked for extra on the mortgage to be able to buy carpets for the new house but they were refused so they went to a different lender.

In 1962 a daughter was born and they called her Michelle. Moya left work at Chilprufe when she became pregnant and did work at home, printing shoe box labels. She also took on a cleaning job at Little Hill Primary School as she could fit this in with her family. In 1965 Nadine was born and the family moved to a bigger house on Dorchester Close. Moya now took on work at home "cleaning cones" as well as working in Atkinson's factory doing "sock turning". She was made redundant when the company closed.

Moya remembers spending holidays with Jack's brother – Brian - and his family, who lived first in Ashburton, then Buckfastleigh and eventually Newton Abbot, in Devon. They stayed on Dada's (Jack's uncle) farm with "huge pigs" which she remembers being as big as donkeys. The journeys were undertaken in the car which Jack owned. They had bought a car from his Dada which Jack had to repair first as it had a broken axle and bald tyres. The Cortina, which Jack later had, kept Michelle entertained on their journeys as she could watch the road passing by through the hole in the floor. That car also had an abandoned apple pip growing in the floor. Jack also owned Cadillacs and Buicks, one of which had been abandoned and was found with bushes and weeds growing through it.

When Michelle was about 15 she met Christopher at a Pentecostal Church outing at Butlins. Jack thought that 'Chris' was a female so Michelle was able to go out with her 'friend' without her Dad objecting. Michelle began work as a clerical assistant with Leicestershire Police preparing evidence for court cases. In 2009 Michelle became ill and her cancer was mis-diagnosed. She broke her arm and bone cancer was then identified. She sadly died aged 49.

Nadine has worked in a number of jobs including in a pie factory, also at Atkinsons and as a bus driver. Her heavy goods vehicle licence enabled her to work as a driver for a telecommunications company but she was injured by an accident with a Moffett digger and was undergoing treatment when she was sacked for not being at work. She is now running her own business providing support for people who have problems with locks and keys. Currently Nadine is buying her own home with a friend to share the costs.

When Jack became a school caretaker the family moved to Narborough for a year but then returned to Wigston. In 1991 Moya began work at Measom Freers on Pullman Road in Wigston and it was there that she met her friend Pam Bradshaw*. Nine years later Moya retired aged 60.

* See chapter on Pam Bradshaw.

When they retired Moya and Pam began to meet for coffee every week. They began to visit Age Concern (now Age UK Oadby and Wigston) to attend the Line Dancing classes, the Tai Chi and decoupage classes. They took over the teaching of line dancing but Moya stopped them all when Michelle became ill. She now enjoys knitting, cross-stitch, puzzles, reading and gardening. Unfortunately Moya was diagnosed with leukemia in 2013 and became quite poorly. During her treatment she lost weight quite dramatically and went from 10stone to 8stone 11 lbs. She is quite healthy now but is still taking medication.

Moya still attends Age UK Oadby and Wigston with Pam and they support the 'Big Knit' by organising the collection of 10,000 little hats for the 'innocent Smoothie' campaign. Many thanks Moya for your dedication.

MARJORIE
HARTSHORN

Marjorie was born to Raymond Hardcastle and his wife Eva (nee Farrar) on 8th March 1927. The family lived in Ossett/Wakefield, Yorkshire. As the oldest child Marjorie was soon followed by a brother, Raymond in 1929 and sisters, Sheila in 1937, Cynthia in 1938 and Janet in 1948.

At the time Wakefield was most famous for its wool mills, coal mines and rugby club. Marjorie's father, Raymond, whilst working in the mines, was also a very good sportsman and excelled at rugby, swimming and cycling. He had a try-out for Wakefield Rugby Club but with a young family to support he was unable to turn professional. There were many happy memories of the Hardcastle family going out for the day on their bikes and some were members of the local Clarion Cycling Club. Marjorie was very pleased that she had been able to cycle for long distances up hill and down dale in the beautiful Yorkshire countryside and often told of these memories when living in Leicester. Especially on one occasion when she and a group of friends cycled from Ossett to Blackpool for the weekend, a round-trip of 180 miles. Later on in life the Cycling Club held reunions for former members and Marjorie was able to attend a few of these.

Marjorie's father, Raymond and her brother Ray.

After leaving school Marjorie initially went to work in one of the many mills around Wakefield. However, she didn't enjoy the factory environment and the noise although she, like the other workers, learned to lip read.

Marjorie's ambition was to become a nurse. She eventually achieved this aim and enrolled on the Nurses Training course at Sheffield Hospital. Her ability to tell amusing stories of her life was put to use when later on she told her own children tales of "Matron" who insisted on no running, correct hospital bed making and a very strict discipline amongst the nurses. The nurses who had trained at the Sheffield Hospital have held reunions in Sheffield. Marjorie and her colleagues from the hospital would get together in a hotel close to the hospital and many very happy hours were spent over a special lunch, chatting and reminiscing about their days as nurses and catching up with their lives since those formative days.

It was whilst a nurse in Sheffield Hospital that Marjorie met a patient who was seriously ill, called Aubrey Edward (Ted) Hartshorn. Romance blossomed between Ted and Marjorie and they married in May 1948. Moving to live in Leicester away from her family and Yorkshire was a big wrench.

The wedding took place in Leicester in May 1948 and it was followed by the honeymoon in Windermere in the Lake District.This became a favorite for future holidays not only for Marjorie but her daughters.

Ted and Marjorie began their married life living with Ted's parents on The Fairway, Saffron Lane. Ted's father was Walter Hartshorn and his mother was Edith May, Edith's family came from Newark. She died in 1955 and only spent a short time with three of her granddaughters. Walter died in 1966.

Marjorie could remember seeing the steam trains travelling to and from Leicester and London racing along the tracks at the bottom of the garden.

During the next three years their daughter Anne was born in June 1949 and Jane in February 1952. Ted and Marjorie's family then moved to live in one of the first council homes built on the new area known as the Eyres Monsell Estate. This was quite a memorable experience for some time as the houses were so new that there was mud and temporary paths everywhere, until the roads and pavements had been completed. Pushing a pram and helping toddler's walk around was not very much fun.

Marjorie gave up nursing when she married but, as the children grew up and went to school, she became the 'Lollipop Lady' at the crossing of Wigston Lane, outside the Montrose Junior School. This was a job which she loved as it gave her the chance to meet people and talk to the children and their parents whilst helping them across the road. She often followed their lives even after they left the school.

Marjorie ensured that there were frequent trips 'home' to her beloved Yorkshire. As soon as the rental car crossed the 'You are entering Yorkshire' sign she would smile and say "The air smells better in Yorkshire." The fact that it was a rental car is quite important to the family history. As the family grew, daughter Elaine was born in 1955 and Lynn in 1956, the journey north became very fraught. All of the children were not used to car travel and often became travel sick at various times throughout the journey. The M1 did not exist and the route took the family past a landmark known as Little John's Well at the side of the road. By the time this was reached the air of Yorkshire might smell better but the air in the car was a different matter. It was necessary to stop at the Well and rinse out the unpleasant containers and have a clean drink. Marjorie also remembered that it wasn't only cars which caused a problem. She reminded her children of the time that one of them was travel sick on the bus to Leicester, along the Saffron Lane, and all of the family had to get off and walk the rest of the way.

Marjorie and Ted holidayed with the girls in a variety of areas of the UK. These were camping holidays and the necessary travel was quite difficult until the girls began to get used to being in a car and the sickness became a thing of the past.

Marjorie didn't enjoy camping and always slept in the car. The family owned their own car by now and she often claimed to know every spring and bump in the seats. On one occasion she was awake early in the morning and saw a submarine sailing along the loch where the family were camped. No-one believed her until the submarine travelled back later in the day. It was during this holiday that Ted could be seen one day cooking the family a meal outside the car on a bleak and rain sodden layby. No-one can remember the meal but the sight of him wrapped up against the rain and the wind didn't help to convince Marjorie that camping was a good choice of holiday.

On another occasion Marjorie and Ted holidayed on a camp site in Wales with their family and the extended family from Yorkshire. The weather was 'quite wet' and as it became clear that the tents were in danger of being washed away it was decided to pack up and return to Leicester. Moving the vehicle out of the sloping field was a source of fun for the children but the adults had to push and seeing them get covered in mud from the churning wheels is a lasting memory. Cynthia never let Ted forget that she was one of the wet and muddy ones when he was quite dry in the driving seat. There seems to be a pattern of rain in these memories.

Marjorie's father and mother, with her youngest sister, Janet, would regularly visit Leicester, sometimes on Grandad's motorbike, with a sidecar. A journey of 90+ miles each way! Marjorie and her children sometimes stood at the junction of Glenhills Boulevard and Lutterworth Road to wave like mad at Grandma and Grandad as they went past in a coach.

Following a short time working at the Leicester Royal Infirmary Marjorie became the receptionist for Dr Hodge, a local GP in the new surgery on the Estate. When the surgery moved, from Sturdee Road to Pasley Road and became a bigger Health Centre, Marjorie moved with the job. She remained there until she retired in 1987, aged 60. This job was perfect for her as she really liked working with people and providing a service to the patients. This became a family joke as she frequently met them in the most unlikely places. She even had a story of being on holiday in Yugoslavia, in a small town square, and a patient came up to say 'hello'. It seemed as if there was "a patient" everywhere that she went.

As her daughters grew up and left home, Marjorie and Ted, with youngest daughter Lynn, eventually moved to live in the Fairfield Estate in South Wigston. Ted had always enjoyed growing vegetables in his garden but now they both became very keen gardeners and enjoyed having trees, shrubs and flowers of all kinds to enjoy all year round. Feeding and watching the birds became very important to Marjorie as she grew older herself.

Marjorie with her daughter Elaine and her children. Twins Charlotte and Ben and Hannah

Marjorie and Ted suffered a very traumatic car accident in 1988 and Ted died shortly afterwards. Marjorie then focussed her attention on her daughters and her grandchildren.

Marjorie had three grandchildren, twins Ben and Charlotte, born in 1982 and Hannah born in 1987. She always enjoyed their visits and has a lovely photograph of them all in the garden with their Mum, Elaine. Ben is now married to Meesong and they have two children, Joshua and Finlay and live in Glasgow. Charlotte and her partner Ben also have two children, Sebastian and Louie, and they live in Leicestershire. Hannah and her partner Ben also live in Leicestershire. Marjorie had to find ways of knowing which Ben was being talked about.

One of the pleasures of the garden became the colour scheme that she chose each year for the hanging baskets and plant pots which she made up herself. Visits to a Garden Centre became very important.

As her health began to deteriorate Marjorie visited Age UK Oadby and Wigston to have her lunch and guess what – she was able to say "Hello" to people there who had been her 'patients'. This time was very valuable to her as she was again able to make new friends and chat with other visitors.

Marjorie died in 2010 and her daughters and her sister Janet returned her ashes to her beloved Yorkshire. She is missed by her family and those who remember being one of "her patients".

JOHNSON

Joan was born in Birstall in 1930, north Leicestershire and was brought up there by her parents – Doris, nee Hanger and Cecil Dalby. In 1934 a brother, Geoffrey was born.

Joan attended Birstall School and Roundhill Community College. Her best friend at school was called Joan Swan and they are still friends now. At the age of 9, they joined the Girl Guides together. As a teenager, Joan also joined the Girls Training Corps where she played the bugle in a band. The two friends had shorthand lessons together and Joan was employed by the end of the course.

Joan left school at 14 and worked in offices from there on, all through the war times. She remembers this very clearly because it was quite traumatising when land mines were being dropped near their home. She remembers having very little food and having to sleep in their lounge under a 'tin shelter' type of protection. Joan's parents found life together very difficult and eventually her father left. Joan can understand why he left but remembers that her Mum didn't cope very well on her own with the children. Meals were not a big feature of their lives and Joan was, at one time, taken into care to "build her up". One of her clearer memories of the war was when she was trapped in a building at work during an air raid. She also notes that she remembers the majority of the men going away to war.

Joan met her husband, Charles, at De Montfort Hall in Leicester when she was 21 during a night out with her friends. He walked her to her bus and they saw each other the next day – she describes it as love at first sight! At this time she was working in an office. Joan and Charles married when she was 25 at the Church in Birstall. Two cousins of Joan were bridesmaids, Kath and Rosemary. The honeymoon was a few days in Ilfracoombe. The new family moved to Oadby where Joan and Charles had a son, Graham born in 1963. Joan was a "career girl" and was 35 when Graham was born.

Joan worked at the British United Shoe Machinery Company but left when she got married. Having taken a course to re-train Joan then went on to be an assistant teacher at Beauchamp College in Oadby as it was nearer to home. Oadby has changed quite a lot since then and she remembers the Council Offices being where Asda is now, the offices are now situated on Station Road across from Abington High School. The Oadby Swimming Pool, however, has always been in its place on Brabazon Road. She recalls Sandhurst Street School that used to be for primary aged children.

One of her favourite memories is of her motor bikes. Joan first bought a push bike. This was new and expensive, it cost her £5 for which she paid weekly and it took a very long time to pay off.

Later Joan bought a Honda 50 which she felt acted as her best friend. She had taken her driving test but failed. Joan's Mum in Birstall was not well and Joan needed to be able to travel to look after her so a motorbike was the only option.

Joan and her husband went on many caravan holidays in their static caravan in Lincolnshire. This was very useful when Graham was young but they finally sold the caravan so that they could take holidays abroad. One holiday that she will remember forever is when they went to Greece in 1992. This is where Charles, 60 at the time, suffered a cardiac arrest so their 4 day holiday turned into 1 month. Joan stayed for the whole time but her hotel booking ended at the end of the holiday so she lived in a very basic bed and breakfast with what Joan describes as "down and outs". As she was spending her days with Charles Joan lived off scraps of food in the hospital. This was a very difficult time and Joan had to cope on her own. It would have been too difficult to get any of her family to visit Greece to help her. Luckily Joan had insurance which covered the costs and helped her to return with Charles when he was discharged from hospital. Joan still praises BA who flew her and the wheelchair bound Charles back to the UK in Club Class.

At last Joan was able to eat as much good food as she wished. Charles had to have a specialist nurse on the flight who helped them to get back to Leicester and settled in at home.Quite a few years ago now, Joan and her husband Charles were going to Belgium so wrote to their local MEP, Sue Waddington, and asked if they could be given a tour of the European Parliament in Brussels. They were escorted the entire time by Sue Waddington MEP and Joan now realises that this was very special as it is not allowed any longer for security reasons. She describes the day as 'very interesting' and 'a very special day out'.

Graham also attended Beauchamp College. Graham worked in a hosiery factory until it closed and he then worked for Leicester City Council as a janitor and he has stayed there ever since. He met and married Rachael and they still live in Oadby. They now have two children; Teresa, born in 1993 and Jessica who was born in 1994. Both of her grandchildren are training to be carers and hope to work with older people when they qualify. Joan sees her family on a weekly basis as Rachael does her shopping.

Charles died in 2000 and Joan has made a new life for herself on her own. Joan eventually sold her home and moved in with Graham and his family for a short time. Finally a bungalow was available and Joan moved to Regent Close. After some time on her own Joan moved to a bedsit in Beech Court. However about 7 years ago, Joan suffered from two very traumatising experiences. One day Joan was getting off the bus in Wigston when her leg got trapped in the door of the bus, meaning she was dragged along the road by the bus. Then, after a few months, she finally made a recovery although this was not for very long as shortly after, when she was walking with her trolley, a lorry reversed and backed into her, sending her flying across the street. These experiences have had lasting damage on Joan as she is still suffering the consequences of the injuries on her legs. Joan moved to William Peardon Court so that she could have a little more support. This was very helpful at first but financial cuts have meant that there is no longer a warden on the premises so the residents need to be more self-sufficient.

Joan enjoys music – her favourite is music of all different languages, especially Greek. Her favourite Greek singer is Nana Mouskouri but singers in many languages are in her collection. This is because Joan feels she picks up languages very quickly so she is able to enjoy the challenge of listening to different words. Joan also enjoys playing bingo at William Peardon Court with the other residents, where she now lives. Joan currently has a ground floor flat to suit her disability.

In 2000 Joan began to feel that she needed some extra support so rang Age Concern in Wigston. (now Age UK Oadby and Wigston) She remembers that a very nice, helpful lady came to visit her and sorted out the problems for her. She also suggested that Joan might like to have her lunch at the Day Centre. Joan attended once to see if she liked it and she has been having her lunch there ever since. A success then! Joan comes to Age UK Oadby and Wigston 5 days a week for her lunch and absolutely loves it! She says that she "couldn't manage without it" especially because everyone is "so good to us".

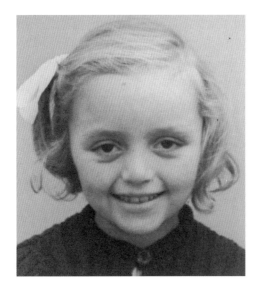

SHIRLEY LEWIS

Shirley was born on the 9th of August 1941 at home – in the front bedroom – in Kingston Avenue, Wigston Fields. Her Dad, Wallace Willis Allen worked for Pickfords heavy haulage. Her Mum, Hilda (nee Bowles) worked in a hosiery factory. Shirley has an older sister born in 1937, called Glenis Kathleen and a younger brother, Rodney Wallace, born in 1944.

Glenis worked in the hosiery industry for many years and is now suffering from COPD as a result of breathing in the fabric dust in the factory. Glenis is now a widow living in Wigston. She has three children, Kevin Tommy Johnston born in 1958 and Kim Elizabeth born in 1961. In 1970 a second daughter, Katherine was born. Kevin lives in Burgess Street in Wigston with his partner and her daughter, Joelle who was born in 1989. Kevin is a lorry driver and recently had to undergo heart surgery. Kim lives in Brailsford Road with her husband Pete Harriman and their children Sean, born in 1998 and daughter Scarlett, born in 2001. Katherine and her husband Gary Weatherall both work in a hospital in Truro, where Katherine works as a clerical assistant.

Shirley and Rod

Shirley attended school in Wigston and has similar memories as Pam Bradshaw* where Shirley also remembers Mrs Outridge. This teacher of needlework also helped Shirley to get her first job. In 1956 there was a great hall where Elizabeth Court is now. Wigston Hall was owned by a family who had a factory in London making luxury dresses.

* See chapter on Pam Bradshaw.

Shirley remembers that she worked on garments for Ascot and other up-market events. Mass-produced clothes reduced the demand for the luxury garments and the Hall closed in 1957. The Hall was finally sold in the early 1960's. Shirley had moved to Graham Gardener, a factory making school uniforms, on Stamford Street in Leicester. After six years there Shirley moved to Kemptons on Belgrave Gate, who produced knitwear.

Shirley then got a job in a big knitwear factory as a secretary. Shirley taught herself to type and worked on invoices and other administrative work. She then moved to Fosse Motors on Hinckley Road. Shirley followed this by working at Corah, where – in 1971 - she met a man who was there to do a 'time and motion' study for the factory. This was Kenneth Lewis, who later became her second husband. When they were courting Shirley and Kenneth enjoyed driving out to pubs in the countryside with friends. Laura and Gordon, who lived in Oadby, and Don and Molly who lived in Narborough.

Shirley and her Dad in 1964

Shirley and Kenneth married in March 1976.

Kenneth's parents suffered some ill health and after his Dad was paralysed by a stroke and his Mum died, Shirley and Kenneth moved in to look after his Dad. Kenneth's father went to live at Curzon House on Humberstone Road where he passed away in April 1976, not knowing that Shirley was pregnant with James, who was born later that year.

The family moved to Wigston in 1980 for better schools. Life was reasonably good although Shirley's Dad passed away in 1980 and her Mum in 1985.

Kenneth himself had a series of minor and one massive heart attack and he therefore had major open heart surgery in 1985. He recovered and was able to return to work until he retired in 1990. Unfortunately, Shirley split up with her second husband in 1991, though they never divorced. Kenneth stayed in the family home and Shirley rented a house in Wigston with her son. As James was then 14 he attended Guthlaxton College and remained there until he was 17.

Shirley met a man who she was with for 4 years until 1997. At this time James decided to move into his own home and at the begining of 2001 Shirley moved into her first flat where she lived for 7 years. In November 2007 Shirley moved to a flat in South Wigston. On the day that she moved Kenneth passed away. In 2012 Shirley moved to Kenneth Gamble Court and is happily still living there independently. When Kenneth died he left James a half share in his house with his half sister. James bought his sister's share of the property and is still living there today. James went back to university in 2012, as a mature student and achived his BA Hons which has enabled him to become a graphic designer in Leicester.

Shirley has been a volunteer at Age UK Oadby and Wigston since 2007 when she worked in reception and in the coffee bar. In 2009 she also began to attend the Line Dancing and exercise classes. Shirley enjoys the social aspect of visiting the center and loves to meet friends and make new friends through her activities. Shirley has also been a very valuable member of the fund rasing team and has supported many events by running various stalls. We are very grateful to her for all of her work and love to see her every week with a bright and cheerful smile.

LOCKWOOD

Joan was born on the 14th of September in 1933 in Goadby, a small village 12 miles away from Leicester. Her parents, William and Gladys Barwell, were farmers. Gladys had been in service in London to Lord and Lady Hazelrigg of Noseley, Leicestershire. William's father had died very young and so William took over the farm when he was 21.

Joan was the oldest child, followed by Kenneth; Robert; a sister, Margaret; then John; Brian and finally Peter who was born in 1943. Her school was at Illston-on-the-Hill, which is closed now. She also attended Church Langton School. Joan was the first pupil to stay on at school until the age of 15. As her birthday was in September she was younger than the other children. Lady Hazelrigg wanted Joan to join the household but as she remained at school Joan was able to work for the family during the school holidays to earn a small wage.

Joan's Mum often shopped at Stoyells in Leicester and when Joan left school her Mum managed to get her a job in the shop. Her salary was £1 5shillings per week, (approx £1.25) while a pair of shoes was about £0. 12s 6d (65p). A shoe shop where the family bought their shoes offered Joan another 5s (25p) per week so she went to work at Briggs Shoes, which is still on the corner of Granby Street. Joan had to cycle to Billesdon to get the bus in to Leicester to get to work every day, more than 5.5 miles, each way.

Joan had noticed a fellow pupil at school called Donald but as he was a couple of years older than her he didn't take much notice of her. However, when they were both at work they began to go out together. They went dancing at Kibworth Village Hall and sometimes at De Montfort Hall where the Ted Heath Band played. Joan probably bought her long dancing dresses from C&A in Leicester. This was where Primark is today and later moved to Granby Street, not far from her work at Briggs Shoes.

Joan and Donald were married at the church in Goadby in July 1955 when Joan was almost 22 years old. Joan's white dress was made for her by a friend. She had two bridesmaids, her sister Margaret and Donald's cousin Mary. They wore gold coloured dresses. The honeymoon was spent in Scarborough, where it rained. The newly-wed couple met Mr and Mrs Lock from Manchester; they were much older than Joan and Donald. The honeymooners didn't tell them that they were on their honeymoon until the end of the holiday.

When they returned to Leicestershire they lived with Donald's Mum in Fleckney for three years after which they moved to Wigston. They still live in the same house now.

Joan worked at Corah's hosiery factory, as an 'examiner' for many years. She left when she became pregnant with Debra. They have 2 children, Debra born in 1962 and Gary born in 1964. Debra works with British Telecom, and lives in Oadby. She has 2 children; Laura born in 1990, and Robert born in 1995. Gary bought the Post office in Lutterworth where he still works. He has one son, Alex who was also born in 1995 and wants to join the police force.

Joan and Donald's grandchildren, Gary and Alex, are only 6 days apart in age; they're like twins. Joan was 28 when she had her first child, Debra, and Debra was 28 when she had her first child, Laura. The second child of Debra, Robert, attended University and studied medicine. He is also very interested in researching into disease. Shortly after entering University he began a career working on cancer. All of the family especially enjoy coming together for holidays and special events.

Donald and Joan, Debra and Gary.

Laura, Robert and cousin Alex in 2000

Joan and Donald have a beautiful small garden at their home. Joan used to bake every weekend and enjoyed making puddings.

Joan and Donald used to enjoy travelling. They have been to Turkey, Spain, Austria, France, Germany, and Italy. For their Sapphire Anniversary (45years) they held a party in their garden and Joan asked everyone to wear blue to celebrate the blue of sapphires. They went to Turkey the first time to celebrate their Golden Wedding Anniversary. All of their family went as well, they booked a special dinner and then a firework display for the children and everybody enjoyed the fireworks on the beach. Their favourite holiday was in Spain.

Back row: Ken, Brian, Robert, John
Front row: Margaret, Peter and Joan
on the 45th wedding anniversary.

For their 50th Wedding Anniversary they invited all of the families for lunch, brothers and sisters, nieces and nephews came in the evening. Debra helped Joan make cakes and everything for the buffet. All the girls stood on the stairs and passed the food up to the spare room. They spent a lovely day. When Joan was 80, the family organised a party at a pub, 'The Horse and Hounds' in Oadby. Debra and Gary did it as a surprise; they booked a table for everyone which Joan and Donald didn't know about. Then on Sunday, the family all arrived secretly to celebrate. They spent a very lovely day together.

To celebrate their 60th Anniversary, their 'Diamond Anniversary' in July 2015 they received a card of congratulation from The Queen.

I am so pleased to know that you are celebrating your Diamond Wedding anniversary on 23rd July, 2015. I send my congratulations and best wishes to you on such a special occasion.

Elizabeth R

Mr. and Mrs. Donald Lockwood

Joan and Donald have been coming to Age UK Oadby and Wigston since they retired. They enjoy meeting friends and having a chat over a coffee a couple of times each week.

Donald age 18 starting his National Service in 1949

DONALD
LOCKWOOD

Donald was born on 5th May in 1931. His parents, Henson and Mabel, nee Barton, lived in Fleckney. Donald was the youngest of their children. Gertrude was the oldest; Ernest, who died during the war; Winnie; John; Audrey and then Donald.

Donald attended Fleckney Infants School and then from age 11 he went to Church Langton School until the age of 14. When he left school Donald began an apprenticeship as a knitter with T.F. Howe. The business was on Oxford Street in Leicester and used to be the site of Walkers pork pie factory. Donald thinks that he probably earned about 25 shillings (£1.25p) per week at the time.

At this time Donald became an important member of the Fleckney Athletic Football Team. He played from the age of about 14 until he went away to do his National Service. He rejoined the team when he returned to England and became the captain of the team, winning many trophies and awards.

Four years later, in 1949 - aged 18, Donald was called up to complete his National Service. He joined the Royal Signals Regiment and served his training at Catterick in Yorkshire. Donald then moved to Loughborough where he was taught Morse Code. This became an important part of Donald's career in the Signals. Donald was then sent to Munster in Germany. Donald remembers that the city was very badly damaged as a result of the bombing raids during the war.

When Donald left the army he returned to work for T.F. Howe's and remained there until he was 27. He thinks that he probably earned about £8 or £9 at this time. He moved to another hosiery company called Woodford's who were based on Mansfield Street. This is where the Leicester City Centre Police Station is now.

Although Donald and Joan* had been to the same school in Church Langton they didn't meet until they began to go dancing at the Palais de Dance in Leicester. In 1952 it cost 2/6d (25p) to go dancing in Leicester although if they went to Kibworth it was cheaper at 2s. (2op) During their courting days Donald and Joan enjoyed going to the cinema and watching Doris Day films. There was a cinema in Oadby and one in Wigston so it was easy to get to from their respective family homes. Donald also remembers that they went to the Palace of Varieties in Belgrave Gate. This was a concert hall where a number of famous variety artists, such as Jimmy Young, entertained the audience.

Having married in July 1955 Donald and Joan lived with his parents in Fleckney until they could afford a house of their own. In 1958 they took out a mortgage of £2,000 with an interest rate of 6% on a house in Wigston.

Donald remembers that he bought his first car, a pale blue Ford Anglia in about 1960. Although he loved the car it was quite old and in those days the three gears did not have syncromesh and he had to 'double declutch'. He kept the Ford for a couple of years before changing the car. He also owned a Hillman Hunter and now owns a Fiesta Automatic.

Donald and Joan love looking after their grandchildren and often take them to the park where they enjoy Donald's trick of saying that he has a surprise for them up his sleeve. His parents used to do this and they are happy to continue the tradition.

Donald visits Age UK Oadby and Wigston for the company and because it has a "nice atmosphere". He sometimes meets an old friend from his working days and even friends from the bowling club. Donald and Joan always know that they can visit and have a chat and a cuppa before getting on with the rest of their day.

VIOLET
MCPHAIL

Violet – known as Vi – was born in the 1920's in Newcastle. At the time of her interview she found it difficult to remember many of the details of her life.

She met her husband Ronald when he was in the Navy. Vi was very proud of the fact that Ronald was a talented artist and she treasured his paintings for the rest of her life. Ronald was a keen golfer and Vi thinks that he would have been pleased that he died whilst playing golf. During the war they lived near London. Vi worked in a munitions factory, putting the caps onto shells. The was quite a dangerous job but Vi doesn't seem to have worried.

When they moved to Leicester Vi became an assistant in various schools and eventually became the Support Technician in the Home Economics Department at Guthlaxton College. Vi enjoyed her job so much that she remained at work until she reached the age of 70. Vi was a talented needlewoman and enjoyed producing clothes for herself. Vi always took care of her appearance and was well known for her very stylish and co-ordinated outfits when she came to Age UK Oadby and Wigston for her lunch. She loved to wear good clothes and matching jewellery and was very rarely seen in the same outfit twice.

Her major talent was in the decorating of cakes. Her fabulous wedding cakes and beautiful sugar craft was something which Vi kept mementoes of until she moved out of her home in Wigston when she needed to live in a residential care home.

Vi was always a very cheerful and sociable person and she was sadly missed when she died in 2014.

MURIEL
MANN

Muriel was born in 1926 in South Wigston. Muriel's cousin, Margaret Lunn became her step sister, as she came to live with them after she lost her parents, but Margaret died at the age of 48 from cancer.

Muriel went to South Wigston Secondary Modern School when she was 11 years old. She made good friends there but most of them are gone now. She also had nice teachers – she clearly remembers her music teacher Miss Holloway, because of the fabulous earrings she used to wear. Her favourite subject was by far Science.

As soon as she left school Muriel started working at a shoe factory, where she was paid £1.00 per week. She then worked in the ATS for 2 years at Desford, but she lived at home so she had to travel there every day. Her salary there was much better as she earned £25 pounds per week.

During the war Muriel's life was seriously affected, as she did medical training and worked with the armed services as a nurse. However, she had to come back to Wigston to look after her mother who was suffering from cancer, and never went back to the war services.

In her early teenage life, Muriel often went dancing, but her father didn't approve of this. She met her husband Peter Mann at the age of 23 in South Wigston. On their first date, she remembers him tipping a glass of beer all over her dress as he attempted a trick. He was a lovely Scottish man who always looked very elegant. It was love at first sight.

After Peter's return from Hong Kong, where he had been for 3 years, they got married and had a "lovely" wedding. Muriel clearly remembers her wedding dress, it was made of silk and had lots of buttons. She had 5 bridesmaids and they had some Scottish traditions in the wedding. On the day Peter gave her a necklace with her initials on it and she has worn it every day since. Their anniversary was on the 14th of March, 1953. They were married for 48 years before Peter passed away, celebrating their anniversary every year. Muriel says, "Meeting my husband was the best thing that ever happened to me" (even though she was always telling him off!). She visits her husband's grave at the cemetery on a weekly basis without fail.

Peter and Muriel had three children; Marlene, who worked as a paramedic for 25 years; Paul, who is a policeman; and Patrick, who owns his own computer business. They all went to Abington High School and Guthlaxton College. Muriel's daughter, Marlene has two daughters. She still sees them quite often as they love reminiscing about the old times and "the good things in life"

Muriel says that Wigston has changed a lot over the years, and that the shops are not as nice as they used to be.

Muriel enjoys watching TV and meeting people. She visits Age UK Oadby and Wigston for lunch and it has been a big part of Muriel's life as she has been coming regularly for 10 years and she "loves every second of it". She has made new friends and loves to come for a chat.

Postscript:-
Muriel became ill and was unable to attend Age UK Oadby and Wigston. Her funeral was attended by some of her friends and we enjoyed the photograph which was featured on the back of the order of service. Muriel loved life and always liked to laugh so this is a great image to remember her by.

In Loving Memory

Muriel Elsie Mann
7th August 1926 ~ 30th May 2016

South Wigston Methodist Church
Friday 24th June 2016 ~ 2.00pm

~~~~

SERVICE OF COMMITTAL
FOLLOWS AT GILROES - EAST CHAPEL
AT 3.00PM

~~~~

MAXTED

Ray was born on 27th September 1934 in County Durham. Frederick and Mary (nee Millar) were his parents. Frederick had been born in 1895. He was very small, possibly 4'4" as an adult, and he wanted to be jockey but he couldn't afford the fee for an apprenticeship so he became a surface coal miner. During the First World War he was in the Durham Light Infantry and was sent to France. The day after he arrived Frederick was hit by a gas attack and was shipped home.

This didn't stop him from smoking 10 – 20 cigarettes a day! He died in 1988. Mary was born in 1897 and worked as a hospital nurse. During the war she was very busy and Ray remembers that when he was very young he went to the ARP Post (Air Raid Precaution) with her and helped to wind and pack bandages. Quite an experience for a ten year old boy. Mary died aged 89. Ray also had an older brother, Ronald who was born in 1924. Ronald was a pilot in the RAF during the war. Ronald married Iris who was in the Air Force as well. During the war years, when Ray was still a little boy, his family experienced frequent bombings as they lived relatively close to the coal mines. Most of his friends were not as fortunate as his family and many of them died during the war.

Ray attended Ryhope Robert Richardson Grammar School for seven years. He remembers his maths teachers, Mr Blenky, Mr Osbourne and the history teacher, Mr McCleod. Discipline was quite strict and Mr McCleod was known to reward bad behaviour with a clip around the ear. When he retired there were a lot of his previous students there so he must have been well respected. As an avid outdoorsman, Ray was the Assistant Scout Master by the age of 17 and later became the Scout Master himself in County Durham.

Ray participated in the weekly meetings and had the responsibility of leading others during their camping and hiking trips in County Durham. Having the passion for helping people and being a very sociable person, Ray was an active member of the Red Cross Society with his mother, for many years, learning about first aid, how to put on splints and bandages. Ray left school when he was 19. He attended the University of Nottingham, where he studied Geology. He claims that he was not a bad student, yet not an excellent student. He was quite an extrovert and enjoyed spending time with friends and organising activities. Instead of his National Service, he signed on for three years and during that time rose to the rank of Corporal in the Royal Army Service Corps which later became the Royal Corps of Transport and has since changed it's name again.

He worked at Imperial Chemical Industries (ICI) as a research chemist for 12 years. During his time at ICI Ray was especiallyinterested in, and was an active member of, the Amateur Dramatic Society and wrote several pantomimes. Ray enjoys sharing his memories of the good old times when he was a dame and wore heavy make-up. He has performed the part of an ugly sister in Cinderella. For several years, he took part in dress and stage rehearsals and performed on stage in front of audiences of up to 400.

Another memorable moment that Ray truly cherishes is of the volleyball competition between the twelve departments at ICI. Ray was really nervous as he got together with several people from the department since none of them knew how to the play the game, let alone what are the rules. Fortunately, a Canadian student, who happened to be an intern there at the time as a researcher, was a volleyball player. The student coached the team every single day for a fortnight before the competition and after a great deal of practice, they would head out and have a pint or two. In the end, they were the best team of the competition and won the championship.

In 1955 Ronald and Iris introduced Ray to a cousin of Iris called Sandra, when Ronald was stationed at Tanmere. Ray was on leave from Wilton near Salisbury and it was a very important holiday. Sandra was 16 and Ray was 21. They married in August 1960. Sandra, a teacher, eventually specialised with 'special needs' children. Hockey and tennis were her sports and she played to a high standard, she still plays tennis.

From left:
Sandra, Ray, Kevin, Ray's Mum,
Sandra's Mum (Mrs Willis), Ray's Dad

Ray and Sandra had three children. Kevin was born in 1961 and now lives in the Algarve. Beverley was born in 1965. She has married Dave and they are living in Weston-Super-Mare with their three children, Bradley (12), Paige (11) and Alisha (9). Ray and Sandra's third child is Hilary who was born in 1970 and she now lives in Amersham, Bucks., with her husband, Brendan and their daughter, Hannah (6). Complete family gatherings are rare though all got together for Ray's 70th and 80th birthday parties.

Ray's 70th Birthday Lunch 25/09/2004
Brendon, Dave, Jasper, Guy, Bev, Gloria, Kevin, Ray, Bev, Hilary, Kevin

Ron and Iris had three children. Gerald was born in 1951 and has moved to the south coast with his wife, Stephanie and their children, David and Helen. Gloria was born in 1953. Ray remembers that she was a "good horse woman" and spent time in social circles with Mrs Betty Skelton (who was a top side-saddle rider in the UK). Gloria married Tony who is a farrier and became Mrs Sleeman-Hiscock.

Gloria worked as the Higher Executive Officer (HEO) to a Brigadier in the army. She lives near Wakefield which is close to her son Jasper, his wife and their three children. She also has a son called Guy who is married to Sabrina. Guy lives near Andover and makes quality oak furniture. Ray enjoys meeting up with Gloria and they spend as much time together as they can. Six years after Gloria was born another son arrived called Michael. He now lives with his wife Lynne and his stepdaughter, Kim in Rutland.

Work at ICI changed as cuts were made to the workforce and promotions became scarce so Ray decided to become a teacher, teaching maths and science for 11-16 year old students in County Durham. Some time later Ray applied for a promotion in Oadby.

When Ray first came to Leicester he was living on his own, until his family could join him. Unfortunately absence didn't make the heart grow fonder and his marriage didn't survive the distance so he and Sandra were divorced in 1978. Ray gained promotion at Sir Jonathan North School. Still teaching maths but also as a Year Tutor responsible for day-to-day discipline. His experience as a Samaritan was helpful when students personal and/or home problems arose. Ray remarried and he and Jean lived in Oadby. Jean was also a teacher and was head of Bilogy. She was also keen on promoting the 'Duke of Edinburgh Award ' scheme. She was invited to Buckingham Palace to receive recognition for the work that she did.

Ray and Jean both enjoyed outdoor activities, often taking his children camping. They, with Hilary and Kevin on occasion, went skiing mostly in Austria. These holidays were for a fortnight or so during the Christmas and Easter holidays and continued for several years. Ray played badminton and was Treasurer for a few years at the Queen's Road Club. Then Ray and his son Kevin took up Tae Kwan Do, Ray gained his Black Belt when in his 50's. Ray and Jean enjoyed going to yoga classes together for a few years. Jean became ill and was diagnosed with multiple sclerosis and polysystic kidneys. Ray took early retirement, when he was aged 54, to care for her. Sadly Jean died in September 1995.

About 1980: Ray, Hilary, Jean

Ray took up English Folk Dancing and was a member of the Burton Overy and Uppingham clubs. He became quite an accomplished dancer and caller. The Uppingham club quite often gave an evening's admission money to charity, eg. Rainbows. Members were invited to dress in the charity colours. For Cancer Research the colour of the evening was pink.

Ray visited Age Concern Oadby and Wigston (now Age UK Oadby and Wigston) and joined the Tai Chi classes for several years, making new friends, whilst still keeping contact with his 'old mates'. In 2005 Ray began volunteering at Age UK O&W and is very dedicated to his responsibilities - not missing the chance to have some fun as well.

Ray had a hip replacement operation in 2012 and quite soon afterwards felt as good physically as he was many years ago. He now limits his exercising to 3 or 4 sessions per week, so he feels that he's not endangering his body. Scrabble, crosswords and brushing up on his German language skills keep his "old brain box going".

Ray is an excellent example of the volunteers at Age UK Oadby and Wigston and we are very grateful for all of his contributions.

Ray's Ode

Said the midwife, "It's well after midnight,
If it doesn't come soon, I shall quit!"
I was born at that unearthly hour,
Half past two and a half and a bit! (2.45am)

_____"_____
Schooling was soon thrust upon me
With examinations to sit
Several "O"'s and some "A" levels
Which were two and a half and a bit!

_____"_____
Then there came National Service.
"Into what regiment would I fit?"
"The Guards" said I, rising to my full height
Five foot two and a half and a bit! (5' 2 3/4")

_____"_____
Came work and eventually marriage,
With a mortgage and family to wit!
Lovely wife, more than average children,
Which is two and a half and a bit! (3 really)

_____"_____
With retirement, I was put out to pasture.
Like a race horse, champing at the bit.
With an eye on my devoted filly
(For the) weekly two and a half and a bit!

_____"_____
The undertaker has his eye upon me,
Measuring my height and my width.
We'll put his remains in a shoe box,
Size two and a half and a bit!

_____"_____
At last I'll meet St Peter,
With him I'll make quite a hit.
"Are there any of my friends up here with me?"
"Only two………………………………!"

MARGARET MOSS

Margaret has been a very important person in the life of Age Concern Oadby and Wigston/Age UK Oadby and Wigston. By the time we interviewed her she wasn't able to remember many details about her life so much of the following information has been collected from articles in the local press and the help of other local residents. Hopefully we can do Margaret justice in return for all of the hard work that she put into her local community.

Margaret was born in Birmingham. She was the youngest of twin brothers Bill and Tom and three sisters - Queenie, Hilda and Joan. Her father was in the Leicestershire Regiment. After World War II her father was transferred to Berlin when Margaret was 16, where he was the commander of the base in Berlin. Margaret would go back and forth from the Russian zone trying to find information on what the situation was like for the people on that side of Berlin. At the end of the war the family lived in London. However, her father was eventually transferred to the Glen Parva Barracks in Leicester and they then lived in Glen Hills, Leicester. Margaret had met an American soldier during her time in London and it broke her heart to learn that he was married. Margaret kept her 'bottom drawer' until her home was moved to the residential care home where she now lives.

The mid 1960's saw Margaret enter the political field as a District Councillor on the Wigston Urban District Council. It was at this point, along with a number of like-minded people that Margaret took up the cause to help older citizens. Wigston's Old People's Association was formed in 1965 (by the Urban District Council) and Margaret was the Honorary Secretary. Margaret was one of the volunteers who helped to cook the lunchtime meals when they were based at the Bassett Centre in South Wigston, before the Paddock Street Day Centre was built.

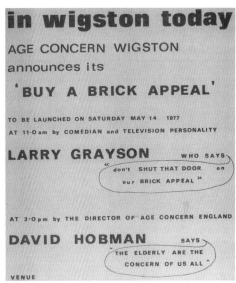

in wigston today

AGE CONCERN WIGSTON
announces its

'BUY A BRICK APPEAL'

TO BE LAUNCHED ON SATURDAY MAY 14 1977

AT 11-0 am by COMEDIAN and TELEVISION PERSONALITY

LARRY GRAYSON   WHO SAYS

« don't SHUT THAT DOOR on our BRICK APPEAL »

AT 3-0 pm by THE DIRECTOR OF AGE CONCERN ENGLAND

DAVID HOBMAN   SAYS

" THE ELDERLY ARE THE CONCERN OF US ALL "

VENUE

In 1977 Margaret launched the 'Buy a Brick Appeal' alongside Larry Grayson.

2 Oadby and Wigston Advertiser, Friday, April 15, 1977

TV star to launch day centre appeal

COMEDIAN and television personality Larry Grayson will launch Age Concern Wigston's brick appeal for the new day centre for the elderly on May 14.

Chairman of Age Concern Wigston, Mr. Alan Kind, said another £10,000 was needed to complete and equip the new centre at Paddock Street, Wigston, and the brick appeal will be the main fund raising event.

Copies of an appeal letter will be distributed in the district during the first fortnight in May. "Already we have £29,500 which is sufficeint for us to complete the structure. Inflation is our problem, the money raised would have been sufficient two years ago," the letter says.

"This is why we have decided to commence work immediately and as the money becomes available so the finishing touches can be added."

A permanent record of all local firms, organisations and individuals who buy a brick will be kept at the day centre. A golden brick will cost £50, a silver brick £25, bronze £5, and copper £1.

The director of Age Concern England, Mr. David Hobman, will be the chief guest at the appeal ceremony to be held at the Paddock Street site.

Larry Grayson was a comedian and television presenter and was very famous in his time. Margaret and her mother were on holiday at a south coast resort and Larry was staying at the same hotel. One day Margaret saw him pacing up and down, and asked him why, to which he replied 'My car has not turned up'. They gave him a lift and he then told her that if there was anything he could do for her she just had to ask, and later there was. Margaret asked Larry to help them raise money for the Paddock Street Day Centre, with one of their primary methods being a door to door £1 a brick sponsorship scheme. Margaret has always tried to make it very clear that she considers Larry Grayson to have been an extremely nice man. We remain grateful for his support.

M.P. cuts first sod for new Day Centre

JOHN FARR, MP for Harborough, launched the [buildi]ng of the Wigston Day Centre for the elderly on [Frid]ay with a turf cutting ceremony.

[The M].P. cut the first turf at [Pad]dock Street site to mark [the beg]inning of work on the [new] building.

[He reco]mmended Age Concern [for tak]ing the initiative to go [ahead w]ith the scheme in times [of tight] budgeting.

[He w]as presented with an [engrave]d spade to com[memora]te the event by Miss [Margare]t Moss, chief secretary [Age C]oncern Wigston.

the Wigston branch, thanked Oadby and Wigston Borough Councillors for making the site available to Age Concern. He said that they had decided to go ahead with the building rather than wait until they had the extra £10,000 needed to complete the interior fittings of the building. "The money we have already would be whittled away by inflation," he said.

Benefit

"I am sure the centre will

John Farr, M.P. for Harborough, cuts the first turf in preparation for the building of a new Age Concern day centre in Paddock Street, Wigston. With him are (left to right) Mr. Harry Lucas, of the Age Concern Wigston committe, Councillor Dr. **nan Reynolds, Mr. Alan Kind, Chairman of Wigston Age Concern, Councillor Walter Boulter, Mayor of Oadby and Wigston, County Councillor R. Curtis Weston, President of Wigston Age Concern, and Mrs Margaret Moss, secretary.

Margaret remained on the Committee as it developed and worked through changes to the facility. In 1971 the name changed to Age Concern Oadby and Wigston and later to Age UK Oadby and Wigston. Throughout this time Margaret remained as Honorary Secretary of the Trustees and later became the Honorary President.

see Appendix A

Margaret loved to drive but was quite impatient with traffic lights and other drivers. She was quite upset when she could no longer drive, although this didn't reduce her independence and she took to walking as often as she could. Margaret was also well known for losing her keys and would eventually need to be supported in either getting into or out of her lovely home.

One of the more recent events which Margaret was proud of was in 2012. To celebrate the Diamond Jubilee of Queen Elizabeth II the Lord Lieutenant of Leicestershire, Lady Jennifer Gretton, identified 60 local charities which she felt deserved special recognition. Margaret was very proud that Age UK Oadby and Wigston received the Award at a special ceremony at County Hall. Following the presentation Lady Gretton visited the Centre for lunch and spoke to Margaret about her work over the years.

Many people have stressed the fact that Margaret was a very caring person who helped people around her when need arose. Her belief in what she was working for was never lost, no matter what she did. It was this constancy which enabled the team of people involved with her to bring about the Centre which we now have.

Margaret remained a supporter of the Age UK Oadby and Wigston and became a frequent visitor, enjoying spending time with her friends for lunch and a chat. She eventually moved into a residential care home but continues to make occasional visits. Thank you Margaret.

see chapter on Kath Carver.

South Leicestershire Crematorium, Countesthorpe

Service of Thanksgiving
for the Life of

Margaret Sylvia Winifred Moss

9th March 1931 - 1st May 2017

Tuesday 16th May 2017
2.00pm

Order of Service

JILL
RAMSEY

Jill was born on 30th July 1940 in a maternity home on Clarendon Park Road in Leicester. Her father, Norman Stafford Curtis and her Mum Vivienne, nee Woodruff Aslett, lived on Victoria Park Road. Jill's brother, John William was born in 1944. Following the bombing on Victoria Park the family moved to Oadby Road in Wigston. The house belonged to Jill's godmother's parents. The Curtis family lived in the boxroom and Jill slept in a hammock over her parent's bed. The story is that if she cried during the night her Dad could reach out with his foot to rock the hammock to get her back to sleep. Eventually they moved to their own home on Brighton Avenue. Jill remembers that at the time there were haystacks on Thorpe's Farm which they could easily see from their home, so it was very much still countryside. Her father often helped local farmers on the Wistow Park Estate by picking potatoes.

During the war Jill's grandfather and his brother were the main beef and lamb buyers at the cattle market in Leicester. Her grandfather, John Curtis, grazed his cattle on the Grange Estate in Wigston and Jill remembers that she learnt to ride on one of the beef cattle. John Curtis was also a professional cricket player for Leicestershire. He played for England against the Australians in the UK.

Whilst still at school Jill often camped at Burrough Court, Burrough-on-the-Hill during the Whitsun holidays. Jill's friend Marion Horlock went with her and the friends travelled there and back in the back of Marion's father's lorry.

Norman Stafford Curtis was a teacher at Linwood School for Boys. In this position he was exempt from serving in the war. In 1946, he became the Manager of the Leicester Schools Football Team. Following this he also took on the role of Secretary to the Leicester Schools Team. His expertise and knowledge enabled him to write the football columns for the Leicester Mercury. He was responsible for the support of the apprentices at Leicester City Football Club and helped them to travel to matches and training sessions. Jill remembers that eventually her Dad helped Gary Lineker, Peter Shilton and Geoff Tate among others. During this time Mr Curtis also began broadcasting the football reports to hospital radio. His first broadcast wasn't very sucessful as, although it arrived at the hospital the broadcast controller didn't connect to the wards and so he was the only one to hear it. Things went better after that. Mr Curtis continued to broadcast to the hospitals until funds ran out some years later.

In 1956 after he became the Headteacher, Mr Curtis was responsible for the introduction of a computer to the school. It was donated by W.D. & H.O. Wills and was a Leo Mark II, the Leo Mark I was installed at the Lyons Cornerhouse in London so Linwood was quite ahead of the computer age.

Mr Curtis also introduced the 13+ examination to the school. Linwood was the first school in Leicester to do this and it provided the opportunity for the boys to take GCE's. Jill remembers that her father also arranged for the pupils to go on educational cruises where they were able to study in special classrooms on board ship.

Mr Curtis left Linwood in 1972, when he became the first Headteacher at a new school called Soar Valley School. The Duchess of Gloucester performed the opening ceremony. On the day there was a bomb scare so the ceremony was delayed. Jill remembers that Mr Curtis had to arrange for there to be a special space made in the ladies toilets for the Duchess to put her handbag.

Jill herself attended Bell Street Primary School where she was taught by Mrs Evans*. Jill then moved to Long Street Junior School where Mr Herrick was the Head Teacher. Upon leaving the Junior School Jill attended Kibworth Beauchamp Grammar School from 1951 – 1957. Her favourite subjects were history, art, music and domestic science.
*see chapter on Peggy Evans

The music teacher at Kibworth was Terry Dwyer who had taught with Jill's father, so she also knew him socially. In 1953/54 Jill joined the Leicestershire County School of Music and travelled to Aarhus in Denmark and Oslo in Norway on their singing trips.

Kibworth Beauchamp Grammar School held a 50 year reunion in 2001 when ex-pupils and staff met up to chat and catch up on their lives. They have continued to hold them regularly ever since although the numbers attending are gradually decreasing. One of the members of Jill's year group is Raymond Bliss who lived in the old cottage on Leicester Road, opposite Brighton Avenue. He has just had his first book published called 'Wednesdays Child'.

Aged 17 Jill left school and went to work at the Midland Bank on Granby Street. She worked on some of the very early computers in the overseas department. She also remembers that they had annual Christmas parties!!!

In 1962 Jill met a young man called John Foster on a blind date. They were married at All Saints Church in Wigston in 1963. John and Jill were on their honeymoon whilst the Great Train Robbery was all over the news.

In 1968 Jill left the bank when her son Stephen John was born. Jill's brother John married Anne-Marie Bell in Leeds the same year. They had met at Manchester University where John studied and gained a PHd in Polymer Technology. He then went to work for ICI in Pontypool. He was later transferred to Harrogate and subsequently he completed a degree in chemistry at London University. He was able to work hard and finish his studies in 12 months instead of the usual 18 months. This led to a job as a Health and Safety Officer in Chester with responsibility for factories in the area, including Runcorn, Widnes and the North East. John and Anne-Marie have four children; Naomi, Jonathon, Sophie and Alex. The family has expanded to include six lovely grandchildren.

Stephen attended schools in Wigston – Fairfield Primary School, South Wigston High School and Guthlaxton College. On leaving school he attended a catering course at Southfields College. (now called Leicester College) Stephen began working for Everards Brewery and eventually managed a pub in Silverstone. Using this experience he, and his wife Helen, began a company selling sandwiches and buffet food including wedding meals. Stephen and Helen have two children, Luke and Holly. He now runs The Bull's Head pub at Clipstone, Northamptonshire, where they have a very successful restaurant and all of his family work together.

Having left her job at the Midland Bank, to bring up Stephen, Jill returned to work in 1974 when she began a part-time job close to home and fitting in with school hours. Jill used this time to attend South Fields College to gain a qualification in soft furnishings. Having completed this she worked for two years at CIS Double Glazing. During this time her marriage ended and Jill supported herself and Stephen by working for Elequip Ltd from 1978 until 1987. One of her responsibilities was to support the paperwork for a colleague who is very dyslexic. Eventually Jill and David Ramsey began to go out together and were married in October 1980. Jill was now 40 years old and had yet to travel on an aeroplane. Her honeymoon flights led to the new family visiting New Zealand, Canada and the USA as well as various places in Europe. They have also been cruising in Alaska to celebrate her husband's 60th birthday.

In 1987 Jill worked for Cromwell Tools as the receptionist and she remained there for nearly 20 years. (7171 days to be precise – according to the inscription on her presentation clock) In 1997 Jill began to raise money for Guide Dogs for the Blind and continues to support the charity, having now raised over £100,000.

Jill retired in 2006 at the age of 66 but she missed the company of others so, hoping to give back to her local community, she volunteered to become a receptionist at Age UK Oadby and Wigston and she has met lots of new friends and enjoys the social life. Jill has subsequently become a Trustee of the charity. Jill has received her ten year certificate. Many thanks for your continued support Jill.

95

EILEEN MARGARET
SALES

Eileen volunteered in the shop at Age UK Oadby and Wigston for almost 20 years. She mostly worked for 2 days per week but could always be relied upon to cover for absent volunteers. Although she didn't want to be interviewed for this book we can't leave her out. I have permission from her son David to publish this short thank you to Eileen.

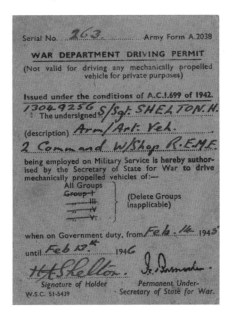

Harry was born in January 1918 as Henry Arthur Shelton. His Mum was called Elizabeth Adams before her marriage. Harry's Dad, Albert Arthur Shelton, was a Coldstream Guardsman and the family lived on Beaumanor Road in Leicester. After his demob from the Army he tried to become a carpenter but became a clicker in the shoe industry instead. After he became fully trained he decided to work his passage to Canada. Elizabeth didn't want to go to Canada so she and the young Harry remained in England. The factories in Canada were making boots for the army so Albert realised that there was demand for ladies shoes. He eventually built a good business making and selling ladies shoes.

At age four Harry went to Belgrave School. When his Grandmother (Adams) took him to school on the first day she told them that his name was Harry Shelton. He has been known as Harry ever since. Harry's Grandmother died in 1925 and she had a funeral with a horse drawn carriage. At age 11 Harry moved to the John Ellis School where he was quite good at French. Harry remembered that the teacher of French was also an organist at the Coliseum in Leicester. During the war Harry's ability to speak French was very useful and he was often called upon to translate for his Captain. The Head Teacher, Mr Young, often talked about skiing holidays in Switzerland. Harry's school was part of St Peters Church.

Harry left school when he was 14, as his father said that he needed to learn to "paddle his own canoe". So Harry trained as a motor engineer. He worked at Parsons Motors in Arborfield, Reading which was owned by Miss Walker who he remembers as a powerful woman. He was soon promoted to foreman. Harry got paid £5.12shillings (£5.75p) per week at this job.

Age 20 or 21 Harry went dancing to the Palais De Dance in Leicester. His partners were often Edna and May. Harry has stayed in touch with them and often met them at Age UK Oadby and Wigston.

Aged 21 Harry joined the Army and worked with No 2 Command Workshop, REME. Eventually Harry was sent out to North Africa, near Tunis. During this time Harry remembered seeing Winston Churchill, Anthony Eden and King George VI when they visited the Tank Regiment. He also remembered the birth of the Princess Elizabeth. Harry also spent some of the war in Italy. He flew from Israel to Naples in an early American aeroplane called a Dakota. It was a goods plane and had wooden seats which flapped up and were attached to the fuselage out of the way. Whilst there he was called into the tent of a Yorkshireman who told Harry that he should be repairing tanks which were needed to be returned to the front. He was sent over the Appennine Mountains to board a destroyer going to Suez. At Tel al Kabir Harry trained other officers, some of them of a higher rank than himself. As a Staff Sergeant Harry was paid £14 per week which was considered to be very good. Harry's work on the maintenance of the tanks has since helped him to work with Major Lidderdale to renovate a Tiger Tank which is now in a museum in Bournemouth.

In 1940 Harry married Margaret Hilda (called Peggy) and they lived with his Mum in Belgrave, Leicester. They had two sons Michael and Neil. By this time Harry and Peggy had bought a house in Cranfield Road in Aylestone.

In 1950/51 The family decided to move to Hillcrest in Bulawayo, the second largest city in what was then called Rhodesia, now Zimbabwe. A third son Gary was born in Bulawayo. Harry worked as an engineer for the Rhodesian Railways Company, Road Transport Service, maintaining the vehicles. After retiring aged 60 Harry went on to lecture at the local college teaching motor engineering. He remained there for twelve years and then became an inspector for the motor industry. Harry finally retired at the age of 84.

During the 50's the family were "in the money" according to Harry. They built their own home which Harry called a villa. They had half an acre of land and employed staff to look after the gardens. A fond memory for Harry is of one of the "boys" - Jotum – said that Harry's car was much too dirty and so he took over the cleaning of the car as well. The house needed a borehole for its water supply and they had to dig down over 100 feet to reach water for the house and garden. Peggy died of cancer in 1960.

In 1964 Gary was attending a Day Centre and this is where Harry met Val, the mother of Grant, and Val took the two boys for days out. Val and the boys went swimming whilst Harry went bowling. Val remembers saying that she didn't mind taking Gary swimming but she objected to paying for his haircuts. Despite this Harry and Val soon became a couple and he remembered taking her to an Independence Day Dance on 11th November 1970. They were married in Bulawayo in 1971.

During the 1970's Harry taught Val to bowl and they became a succesful team, winning the Hillside Cup Mixed Pairs trophy in 1996.

Unfortunately Harry died in 2014 so Val has completed the story.

Val remembers that they had a nice life in Bulawayo. In 1975 Harry and Val came to Leicester to visit Harry's mother. On their return they took her back for a holiday. During her stay they all celebrated her 80th birthday, with Harry's friends from the bowls club. The visit was intended to be for three months but she became homesick and so came back to Leicester after two months. Harry and Val came back to Leicester in 1979 and also visited friends in Germany. A friend looked after the two boys so that Harry and Val could travel around more easily.

Life in Zimbabwe became very difficult for the family with food shortages and having to queue for bread and milk. In 2004 they decided to move back to England. It was quite difficult to sell their property as no-one was able to pay the real value. Eventually they managed to sell with enough money to help them to re-locate in England. Harry's son Neil was living in Durban at this time. His other son, Michael and his two sons Ryan and Adam were already living in London so helped to look for a house for Harry and Val. Michael's wife, Thea and their daughter Shelley stayed in Bulawayo until Shelley had completed her exams in December 2004.

At first Harry and Val lived with Harry's pre-war friends in Oadby. Anne Shilton and her sister were very helpful and took the new arrivals to the council and within two weeks they were able to move into bungalow.

Val's son Grant was still living in South Africa but, in 1995, he was an innocent bystander when he was caught up in a bottle store robbery where he was shot and killed. His wife and their children, a son called Keaton and a daughter called Tayla, now live in Perth, Australia.

Harry and Val began to visit the Age UK Oadby and Wigston Day Centre on Friday each week to meet with friends and have a coffee and chat. This helped them to widen their social lives as Harry had now become blind. Val recalls "very nice people" at the Centre and they both enjoyed their visits.

We are glad that you found new friends and nice people here Val.

HEATHER
SPENCER

Born in Melton Mowbray in 1937, Heather had an identical twin and later a younger sister called Christine. She also had a step brother, Anthony. They were all schooled in Melton Mowbray, and in 1942 they all moved to Swindon as her father was in the army and was transferred. Unfortunately her twin died as a result of the war in Swindon, after which her mother moved back to Melton.

However, when Heather was five years old her father was transferred to Kent and so Heather went with him and lived in Folkestone for a few years. After the war the whole family moved to Aylestone in Leicester. Unfortunately soon after the move her mother fell ill, at age 41, and Heather had to go to Bedfordshire to live with her aunt and uncle. Heather was aged 12, she remained there until she was 18.

After Heather moved back to Leicester, she got a job in a factory on Narborough Road, where she met her first husband, Eugene. She worked there for two years until they were married, after which they had five children; Ann-Marie, Michael, (who passed away in 2009), Jo, Bernie and Genie. To Heather's great delight she has 15 grandchildren and 15 great grandchildren. They all live in Leicester so the family is very close.

After 19 years of marriage, Heather divorced Eugene after she found out he was having an affair. Her divorce left her on her own looking after the children. She managed to support her family by working in a hosiery factory as an over-locker/machinist for 9 years. She also worked in a laundry and valeting cars for local car sales companies. She worked hard and was able to pay for the weddings of her children.

Heather makes friends very easily and in 1986 she met Trevor on a blind date. Their first date was at the Wheatsheaf in Swithland. She was told to wait for him to pick her up in his car and it began to throw it down with rain, soaking her to the skin, she still waited and luckily Trevor arrived on time. He had brought her a packet of cigarettes to be courteous and gentlemanly. Unbeknown to him, Heather had recently given up smoking! They married after only a few months and their anniversary is on 14th June and they would have been married for 29 years in 2015.

Heather and Trevor have had a very happy marriage, even if she did wait for Trevor to fall asleep and then would wake him up for a cup of tea! Heather loved going out for meals and to shop, particularly in Market Harborough or Melton Mowbray. She loved dancing when she was younger and enjoyed going to The Palais in Leicester. Another passion were the family caravan holidays and especially going to 'Skeggy'. Heather loved spending time with her grandchildren and was very proud of their achievements.

Gardening, knitting, crochet and making all sorts of things kept Heather busy and happy and she once won an Easter bonnet competition. She enjoyed collecting ornaments and in particular dolls and dolls' house items. Heather also had a love of animals and has cared for cats and birds but mostly her dogs. She owned Yorkshire Terriers and her last one was called Tara.

'Coronation Street' was very important to Heather and she wouldn't miss an episode! A fond family memory of Heather is her habit of swapping furniture; settees and coffee tables with friends. Heather has been described as a beautiful lady who always looked glamorous. She liked dressing smartly and always had her make-up on and she loved buying new clothes and shoes.

With five children to look after Heather needed to be quite strict. Her family remember that she could be fiery and feisty. Heather would speak her mind and she would let you know her opinions. She insisted that the family sit down together for Sunday dinner. If you visited Heather she would invariably ask "Have a cob or some cake?". Heather and Trevor enjoyed visiting Age UK Oadby and Wigston and was well known in Wigston where she had many friends.

Since beginning this interview Heather suddenly died. We have permission from her family to use her eulogy and the photograph of her from the Order of Service.

A SERVICE TO CELEBRATE THE LIFE OF HEATHER SPENCER

16TH APRIL 1937 – 13TH MAY 2015

The South Leicestershire Memorial Park & Crematorium
28th May 2015

Poem read by Kayleigh Hawkes at the funeral of her Grandma, Heather Spencer.

Poem for Grandma

Sleep now Grandma
Although we cannot see you,
We feel your presence near
We will hold you close in memory
Till we drop our very last tear.
So sleep now with the angels
And your golden heart let rest.
Although our hearts are broken
We know God only takes the best.
So dance beyond those golden gates
And although this pain is painful
And we really don't wanna let you go
We will wait for the time when we all
Dance beyond those golden gates
So together one day we will glow.
Until that day we close our eyes and see
your smiling face
I'll lock you up inside my heart,
Until we meet again.
So rest now Grandma
I'll never forget you,
Sleep now in the sun.

TREVOR BERT
SPENCER

Trevor was born on Christmas Eve in Leicester.

As a teenager he did his National Service as a driving instructor in the army. He continued this into civilian life and spent some time as a driving instructor. Trevor also worked as a gas engineer for many years.

Trevor married and had three children; Kevin, Paul and Janet. Sadly Trevor and his wife went their separate ways and Trevor lost touch with his children.

However, in 1986 he found love when he met Heather. Their first date was at the Wheatsheaf pub in Swithland. During their courting days Trevor had to ring Heather when he got home to let her know he had arrived safely. They married and Trevor gained a new family with Heather's five children; Ann-Marie, Michael – who sadly passed away in 2009 – Jo, Bernie and Genie. Trevor and Heather went everywhere together, especially to 'the club' on Saturday nights. They owned a caravan for a time and enjoyed their holidays. Trips to Skeggie were a favourite and the family have many stories to remember these holidays by. One story is about a caravan holiday at Richmond Park in Skeggie and having been out for a drink Trevor and Chris were trying to buy chips... (the family know the rest of the story!) Scampi and chips were Trevor's favourite and he liked to order what he called his "cappatino with choc choc". He is also remembered as liking a glass of whiskey. Heather and Trevor liked to go out for a meal and spent time going from cafe to cafe in Wigston.

Trevor liked to make good deals and enjoyed going to car boot sales and second hand or charity shops looking for a bargain. He liked to use his gadgets; 'phones, cameras and watches and he was also "mad" about cars. Trevor loved to watch wild birds and, after Heather passed away, he enjoyed going fishing.

Heather had begun to make decoupage pictures and Trevor tried one of a Mosquito aeroplane. Trevor's job at home was to keep the gardens neat and tidy and he took pride in this. He has been described as hard working, he was a proud and faithful man who rarely lost his temper. He could however, be grumpy and if you were talking to him he would just change the subject.

The family has grown and there are now grandchildren and great grandchildren. Trevor's family also includes Tara, a dog. He wasn't too keen on walking Tara so when she had done what she needed to do he picked her up and carried her home.

Trevor and Heather were very happy together although they did have 'their moments'. They enjoyed visiting Age UK Oadby and Wigston where they met new friends. It was hard for Trevor when Heather died in 2015. Eventually he did start to get used to independent living and he met a lady called Mary. They became close friends and Trevor looked after her when she was hurt in a car accident. They both visited Age UK Oadby and Wigston and continued to enjoy the friendships which they both had there. A lasting memory of Trevor for his family are his sayings. "There's only one thing" or "I know what I meant to tell ya". (I hope that he would be pleased with what we have told ya.)

A SERVICE TO
CELEBRATE THE
LIFE OF
TREVER SPENCER

24TH DECEMBER 1936—17TH JUNE 2016

THE SOUTH LEICESTERSHIRE MEMORIAL
PARK & CREMATORIUM

12TH JULY 2016

Back row: Betty, Glenys and Ken   Front Row: Joan and Margaret

EILEEN
TOACH

Eileen was born on 17th March 1929 at home on Curzon Avenue in Aylestone. Her Dad was Albert Dilkes and her Mum was Catherine, nee Smith. Eileen is the sixth of their sixteen children.

Leonard was born in 1918 but sadly died in 1920. Beryl was born in 1920; Cyril in 1922; Joan in 1924; Ray in 1927; Sidney in 1925; Norman in 1930; Gordon in 1931 and died aged 43; Glenys in 1932; Betty in 1933; Ken in 1935; Shirley in 1936 Margaret in 1939; twins Gillian and Wendy in 1943.

(see chapter on Glenys Wilkinson)

The family moved to one of the newly built houses on Lansdowne Grove in 1940. Eileen remembers that when she was aged 4 she went to the nursery at St Thomas's Church Rooms. This clearly made an impression on her as she remembers being allowed to go to sleep every afternoon. Aged 5 Eileen then went to the Bassett Street Infant School. The memory from here is of the school sending them to the dentist, which the children enjoyed as they were given sweets as a reward.

At the age of 11 Eileen attended the Sir Jonathan North School for Girls. This is where Miss Bassett and Miss Judge taught PE and Eileen learnt to swim. Her friends were Jean Brown, Shirley, Joan and Betty. Eileen remembers that as she had six sisters she was not allowed to "stray" so was very well behaved. When Eileen was aged 14 she went to the Knighton Fields Road School Youth Club which was held from 7pm – 9pm. She enjoyed dancing, snooker, volleyball, darts and table tennis. They held mixed competitions with the boys and this led to a few romantic relationships! During the evening they were able to enjoy a "cuppa and a cheese cob" and a "chat with the boys"!

Eileen left school aged 14 and trained as a tailoress at Welford Dresses, a company set up at the back of the properties on Welford Road, near the prison. Eileen describes the building as "a little shed, up some rickety wooden stairs". The manageress was Miss Clarke who was "very strict but it was really good training". Eileen worked Monday to Friday from 8am - 6pm, with one hour for lunch. On Saturday her hours were 8am - 12 pm. Having worked 49 hours per week Eileen was paid 17shillings and 3d. (Approximately 78pence!

One of the memories which Eileen has is of making some grey jackets. It was only after she had finished them that it was noticed that the fabric was different shades of grey. Eileen was told off but she stood her ground and said that the cutter should have noticed the problem when cutting the fabric. As a consequence of her arguing back Eileen was suspended for three days without pay.

Eileen and her friends sometimes went to the cinema in Leicester. Freemen's Common was close by Welford Road and at lunchtimes Eileen and her friends at work sometimes went scrumping for fruit to eat at the cinema. The cinema was the Odeon on Queen Street (where the Athena nightclub is now). The films did not have sound so there was an organ which rose up from the floor, and the organist played appropriate music to accompany the film. The cost of the best seats at the cinema was 9d (approximately 3p) but if they went to the 'Saturday Rush' in the afternoon it cost 3d (approximately 1p). Eileen remembers the Roy Rogers and "Lone Ranger" films which were cowboy stories. Sometimes it was possible to go to the toilet from the cheaper seats but go to the expensive ones when you came back.

At home the family always sat at the table for their meals. On Sunday nights they would listen to the 'wireless' and have a treat of drinking a fizzy drink - everyone called it 'pop' then - called dandelion and burdock. A lorry travelled around the streets selling the drinks from the back of the lorry. It was good because you didn't have to carry the heavy glass bottles back from the shops. As the bottles were expensive they included a small amount which you could get back if you returned the bottle. (The early life of re-cycling!)

Eileen thinks that she was quite a 'tomboy'. By the time she was 17 she had met a young man called Alan who "admired her but was frightened to meet her". When they did start to spend time together he decided that she was nicer than he thought! They started 'courting' (dating) in 1946 when Eileen was 17. Alan Toach was her only really serious boyfriend. He walked miles every time he visited her. Alan was a keen amateur photographer and has taken some lovely pictures of Eileen and all of her family. In 1951 he took a very glamorous picture of Eileen which she still likes to look at.

During the Second World War Alan's Mum had six sons in the fighting; all of them came home. When he was 18 Alan followed his brothers and served his National Service in the Royal Signals in the Army. His barracks were on Station Road in South Wigston. Eileen cried all night when he left as she thought that South Wigston was a long way from Aylestone. He was then sent to the base at Catterick and it was there that he learnt Morse Code. One of his brothers, Cyril was a Sergent Major at Catterick and came home more often than Alan so Eileen remembers giving him 5shillings (25pence) to take back for Alan so that he could buy shoe polish and treats. Alan's brothers helped him to work through the Army systems and taught him how to starch his collars. When Alan "passed out" - left the army training course - he was the Best Dressed Soldier. During his army service Alan was posted to Palestine where there was a war during 1947/48. It was during this traumatic time that a close friend of Alan's was killed. Alan was very upset and he became very anxious and often felt unsafe. Alan began to smoke as a result of this experience. Eileen and Alan were separated for eighteen months whilst he was away. When Alan left his two years of National Service he was offered a job with Reuters or continue in the army and train as an officer. Alan wanted to come home to his family so returned to Leicester.

On 23rd February 1952 they were married at 3pm. Alan and Eileen were both 22 years old. Eileen wore the dress given to her by Joan, her older brother Ray's wife. It was made from a heavy grosgrain embossed fabric and was an "Edwardian" style, collared, ankle length white dress with long sleeves which had pointed cuffs. The dress was eventually passed on to her sister Glenys, and then to her sister Shirley. Eileen had four bridesmaids - her sisters Margaret and Shirley and Alan's sisters Annemarie and Judith. They wore white dresses with cherry red trimming and muffs.

Annemarie enjoyed swimming and one day she was promised that a relative would take her and the twins to Knighton Fields Baths. The relative didn't arrive so Annemarie went to look for them. She was in a hurry and ran across the newly made zebra crossing. Sadly she was hit and killed by a bus aged just 10 years old. Her grandmother was so shocked that she didn't speak for a week.

Eileen and Alan went to Lynmouth for their honeymoon. Alan wanted to treat them so he paid for First Class tickets on the train. However, they missed their connecting train in London by four minutes and so didn't get their First Class seats. On the journey back home they sat in the cheaper seats and had to be reminded that they should be in First Class.

As a married couple they first lived on Cavendish Road in Aylestone. Eileen says that they were an "old fashioned" couple and they chose not to have children until they were able to buy a home. They were married for seven years before they moved in to a house on Mere Road and children began to arrive. Karen was born in 1959 and Richard in 1962.

For the first two years of her married life Eileen continued to work but then took time off. During this time Eileen was making the clothes for herself and both children and was able to make use of her tailoring skills. However when the children went to school Eileen wanted to go back to work. She found a job as a school dinnerlady at Glenmere Primary School. This enabled her to be at home for her own children. Eileen stayed at Glenmere for six years and describes this as "absolutely fabulous". Many of the children that she knew then still recognise her and speak to her. Eileen then worked for Ladies Pride on Bull Head Street as a seamstress, again using her considerable skills. This was a family business and Eileen enjoyed the friendships and happy atmosphere there. Ladies Pride was a good firm to work for and Eileen stayed for 23 years before she retired aged 68.

When the children were young Alan and his brother bought a new car each. Alan drove the family to the French Riviera with Eileen's sister in law, her husband Eddie and their small daughter, On the way south the weather was very bad so they changed direction and went to Spain instead. The road was only a B road and the conditions were "atrocious", winding through woods, trees, more trees and deep drops on one side of the road. Alan eventually had to stop driving as he was too frightened to carry on. Eddie got out of the car and walked in front to check the road. They then drove a few more miles and then stopped again. This went on all day and the journey took eighteen hours. They had never experienced an electric storm before and it was quite frightening. As it was very dark they decided that as everyone was very tired but ok that they would all sleep in the car. When they woke the next morning there were lots of people looking in the windows at them – they were parked on the beach! Despite the language problems everyone had a good laugh about this. In total the holiday driving had clocked up 2,000 miles. After all of this they got lost in London on the journey home. (Obviously a memorable holiday.)

When Richard was 10 years old Alan started his own football team. All of the family went to the matches and shouted out the names of the team all through the game. Eileen remembers it being emotionally exhausting. Karen told her Mum that one day at school someone asked her if the football team was her Dad's. When Karen said it was they said "must be your Mum on the side with a big gob!" (The fact that Eileen is happy to tell this story shows what a wonderful sense of humour she has.)

Karen left Guthlaxton College aged 18 and went to work as a PA at Admiral clothing in Wigston. She eventually left to work with one of the buyers who set up his own business and Karen has worked in all aspects of his business.

Richard left school aged 16 and has worked in a variety of jobs leading up to now working at Walkers Crisps and Eileen thinks that they are a very good firm to work for.

Eileen loves meeting people so she still comes to Age UK Oadby and Wigston to meet friends and family. She has described it as "A wonderful place, tell everybody to come, it's like our front room. We can share our trials and tribulations without being nosey."

Thank you Eileen, you have been a treat for us as well.

Back row: Shirley, Betty, Glenys, Eileen.
Front Row: Wendy, Margaret and Gillian

Bob and Ann

ROBERT EDWARD
TWAITS

Robert Edward Twaits was born on 16th August 1938 in a hospital on Bond Street in Leicester. It isn't there anymore and the Leicester Tax Office is now almost on the same site. His parents were Percy (Bob) Twaits and Alice (nee Jenkins). Bob has a younger sister called Ann.

Bob's parents were both 'in service' at a big house near Stamford, and that is how they met. His Dad was from Ipswich and his Mum from a village near Burton-on-Trent..

When Bob's father left school aged 14, he went to work in a school, cleaning the children's shoes and looking after the buildings. He then went to work on the railways and this is when they moved to Leicester. The job was in South Wigston, which had its own station then. When Bob was born the family were living in Highfields, in Leicester. It was a long way for his Dad to travel so they moved house to Lansdowne Grove, in South Wigston. Bob remembers that the week after they moved out of the house in Highfields the building was bombed. A lucky escape for his family.

Bob still has his gas mask from the war and as it was for a child his is a Mickey Mouse one. Bob remembers that whilst he lived in South Wigston there was a camp for prisoners of war. They worked on the building of the roads around Central Avenue. The local children often spoke to the prisoners even though they didn't share a common spoken language. Bob remembers that signs easily overcame the language problems. The prisoners were held behind fences in the park where the children played. The prisoners carved scraps of wood into little toys during their spare time and they gave them to the children.

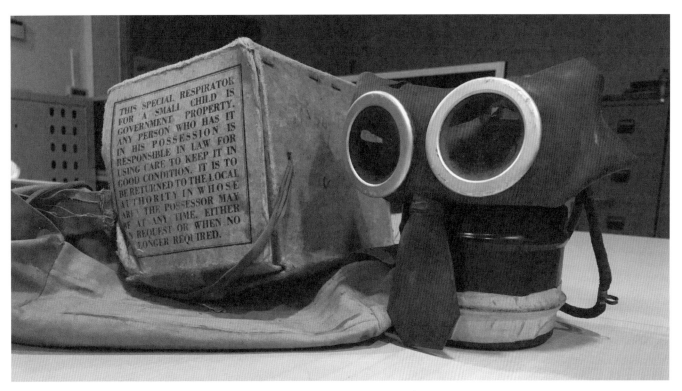

Bob's Mickey Mouse gas mask

Bob's father's job was shunting the engines and carriages from one place to another and sometimes he would take Bob with him. Bob remembers one time when his father let him stand in the engine drivers cab and he showed him how to load the coal into the engine. During this time Bob's mother had a job as a cleaner for a private house on Welford Road. She later worked in a factory making boots and shoes and for a while she worked in a hosiery factory. One of the factories was on West Avenue in Wigston.

Bob's memories of living in the council house on Lansdowne Grove are not very happy. He lived with gas lights and cockroaches. Bob also recalls that he attended the Congregational Chapel from the age of 4 until he was about 18. He still has his Bible from that period.

The family were very glad when they could move to a 2 bedroomed terraced house on Leicester Road. The row of houses were called the 'Tenrow' and this refers to the fact that there were ten houses and is not the actual address. There were more than one 'Tenrow' in Wigston.
(see chapter on Pam Bradshaw)

The houses on the left is where Bob lived.

Another Leicester Road photograph taken in the 1930s. The building in the distance has a large sign advertising that Mitchells and Butlers ales and stouts are sold there. Further on a house stands on the site of the present Bishop & Bishop's Garage.

Bob was probably about five years old when the family moved. These houses don't exist anymore but they were somewhere near where The Bell pub is now. There was a terrace of five houses with a passage between three and two. The toilets were in the back yard and they had to share with the neighbours. The toilet paper was newspapers cut up into squares and hung on a nail in the wall. This house was much better and his father had electricity put in for the downstairs rooms and the parent's bedroom. Bob was about eight years old when he first used electricity. Bob's bedroom didn't have electricity so he still had to use a candle. He also remembers that the windows were often iced up in the winter, sometimes inside as well as outside! Bob's father used to put his big railway coat on Bob's bed to keep him warm at night. He also remembers using the 'pot under the bed' at night (these were called the 'guzunda' because they go under!) rather than going out into the cold to the toilet. When the electricity was installed Bob liked listening to 'Dick Barton' and 'Journey into Space' on the wireless, as the radio was then called.

When Bob lived on Leicester Road, he says that life was much safer. People could leave their doors open and not worry about crime. One of his memories is of the cows walking through the village and the horse and cart delivering the milk and ice cream. He remembers his father sitting him on a cow. The family also owned some chickens and Bob recalls having to teach them how to perch at night, lifting them onto the perches again and again until they knew how to do it. At the back of the houses there was an orchard and the children often went scrumping.

When Bob first went to school he went to a nursery on Central Avenue. This was because both of his parents worked and he was looked after at the nursery until his mother came home. When he was five Bob went to the Infants School on Bell Street. Sainsbury's have built their store on this site. He remembers one of his teachers called Mrs Evans (also known as Della from her show business career) *(see chapter on Peggy Evans)* and he now sees her daughter at the Paddock Street Age UK Oadby and Wigston Day Centre. Bob clearly remembers that as a child their Christmas presents were a sock with an apple and an orange in it! That's all they received. One year they had a chicken for Christmas lunch and when it arrived at their home it was too big for the oven. Opposite to their house was a bakery called Hilton's (where Gregg's is now) and they had large ovens so quite a few of the local residents took their Christmas birds to the bakery to be cooked.

Just after the war when Bob was about eight years old he had a new teacher who arrived from Canada and brought presents for all of her pupils. Perhaps as it was so close to the end of the war she thought that they wouldn't have had many treats. Bob received a plastic fire engine with a ladder, a moving wheel and a fireman. This was the first plastic that Bob had ever seen. Bob still has the fire engine.

On one occasion when Bob was ten years old he was climbing a tree, to collect wood for a fire to cook potatoes, when the branch broke and he fell and broke his arm in two places. After treatment for the broken arm Bob went home and seemed to be alright but soon fell into a coma which lasted for three days. Whilst in hospital again it was diagnosed as a diabetic coma and Bob and his family were told that he had been very close to dying. Bob has been determined not to let the diabetes affect his life. He doesn't miss eating sweet things as he has never eaten them as they weren't available during the war. "You don't miss what you've never had." Bob needed to have two injections every day and to begin with he was too frightened to inject himself so his Mum did it for him. The needles were very large and had to be sharpened regularly by the local chemist. He now uses smaller needles himself for the four injections which his condition now requires.

Living on Leicester Road meant that they lived opposite a chip shop and it was possible to go in to ask for scratchings – bits of cooked batter – which they gave away for free. There was also a newsagents called Wiggintons. Bob tried to get a paper round at the shop but too many people were asking as it was a good job for a child to earn pocket money. Bob did have 6d (about 5p) per week pocket money and he spent it on buying the Beano and the Dandy as they were his favourite comics. He also has memories of Charlie Moore's music shop. Charlie Moore also had a band which played for the parades and festivals in South Wigston and Wigston Magna. One of the parades featured a float for the St John's Ambulance and his sister, Ann was on the float as it travelled from the Co-op on Bell Street through the streets of Wigston. Bob bought his first record from Charlie Moore's shop, it was an Al Jolson LP.

Bob and his friends often went to the canal to swim and play. He had hand knitted swimming trunks and when they got wet they were not easy to wear! Bob also remembers that as a child he was able to watch films because the Co-op on the corner of Central Avenue issued free tickets to children. He also remembers that there was a Salvation Army centre on Bull Head Street and he was able to watch 'Felix the Cat' films for 2d (less than 1pence).

When he was eleven Bob attended the school in Long Street. This is the one where the Records Office is now. At the Long Street school Bob might have had a hard time concentrating because his art teacher wore very short skirts and low cut tops. She was a French lady and obviously made a big impression on Bob! The Headmaster was Mr Kind and his nephew is Alan Kind who is a very well-known Wigston historian, and a Trustee of Age UK Oadby and Wigston.

(see Appendix Timeline)

The last school that Bob attended was Long Street Secondary School. Mr Harrison taught Bob woodwork but he doesn't remember any of the other teachers, perhaps they didn't wear short skirts! He does remember cutting up a frog in Science lessons and he is proud that he came second in his year in science.

The railway company had used a lot of bicycles during the war, painted in camouflage colours, and afterwards they sold them off. Bob's father bought one and painted it black and gave it to Bob for his 14th birthday. Bob's sister also had one. His Dad paid 2/6d each for them (approximately 25p each).

Ann, his Mum and Bob

Bob left school at 15 and went to work at Corah's making ladies stockings. Bob had been offered the choice of two jobs with Corah; one was shift work as a mechanic and the other was day work as a counter hand, sorting socks into good and seconds. Bob sensibly chose the day time work. He stayed at Corah for 21 years before being made redundant.

Bob wasn't able to do his National Service because of his diabetes. He wished that he could have joined the army with his friends and feels that he might have missed out on that experience with them.

When he left Corah he went to work for Pecks, another factory and he worked there, on West Bridge for 25 years. They were also a hosiery factory and the building is now flats. The factory building was damaged by fire and therefore the company moved to Aylestone Road on the site where ALDI is now. Eventually Bob was again made redundant. He then worked for Invicta Plastics where he earned £3 per hour. As a very sociable person Bob enjoyed work as he was able to combine both the social and practical aspects of working in a large company.

Bob bought a Vespa scooter when he was 18 years old. He went to the house where the owner of the scooter lived which was opposite the Race Course in Oadby. Bob didn't recognise the man who turned out to be a footballer with Leicester City. He bought his first car when he was 25 years old. It was a black Hillman Minx. Bob also began ballroom dancing lessons aged 18, at the Trocadero in Leicester. He was very good and won trophies and other awards. He continued to dance until he was about 25 years old.

Whilst working at Corah in 1968 Bob had met a lady called Jackie who also worked at Corah in the training centre on Sanvey Gate. Jackie offered to help Bob, who lived on his own, by cooking for him. They 'courted' for four years before getting married. They enjoyed ice skating in Nottingham, dancing at The Palais in Leicester as well as at The Granby and a dance hall above a shop at the bottom of Charles Street. They were married on 3rd April 1972 at the Leicester Registry Office when it was opposite the Cathedral. Jackie wore a navy coat and dress with a navy hat.

They then lived in Bob's home in Wigston. He had bought the house for £3,000 and was able to afford the mortgage on his own before he married Jackie. Bob doesn't like to be in debt.

Bob remembers that his first holiday abroad was a train journey to Italy. They travelled by train to Victoria Station in London, then by train to Dover where they took the boat train across the Channel and down through France, Switzerland and in to northern Italy. On the same holiday they met a couple of 'girls' who had also travelled from Wigston. One of the girls was the daughter of the family who owned Voyles shoe shop in South Wigston. In 1964 he and his friends drove to the south of France and into Spain, in the Hillman Minx. The car broke down in France and Bob called the AA in England who arranged for the local French garage to repair the car and get them back on their journey.

Bob and Jackie love foreign holidays. They have often been to Italy and Greece. Their favourite destination is in Rhodes and they have been returning to the same resort for seventeen years. They now leave a bag of their belongings at a flat owned by a friend there to save them having to carry it back and forth each year.

Jackie worked at Angel Hosiery on Oakland Road in Leicester and for the last three years before his retirement Bob also worked there. They then retired together in 2003.

One of Bob's neighbours asked him if he would like to share an allotment near to his home. He has enjoyed growing beans, potatoes, 'sprouts and leeks – no flowers. Bob now finds that the heavy digging is getting harder as it is very tough ground. He may be forced to give it up in the future.

Following her retirement Jackie volunteered at Age Concern Oadby and Wigston (now Age UK Oadby and Wigston) in the shop. Bob came to the centre with her and helped to sort the bags of donations. Eventually he began to work in the coffee shop on Saturday mornings and often covered when people were away on Friday afternoons. They have been visiting Age UK Oadby and Wigston since 2004 and Bob and Jackie enjoy the social life of the shop and the coffee shop. Meeting with old friends who come to the Centre gives them a chance to catch up on gossip.

One of the responsibilities which Bob took on was to collect toys which had been donated to the shop but were in poor condition. He took them home, cleaned them and repaired them, fitted new batteries where necessary and sold them at the Christmas Fair which was held every year in the Centre. He loved doing this and is proud of the work that he was able to do to help raise funds for the Centre. Many thanks for your efforts Bob and the time which you have spent supporting the charity.

A U D R E Y
WAIN

Audrey was born in Bond Street Maternity Home to James William Langton and his wife Louisa Matilda (nee King) on 25th January 1928. She was their oldest child. Twins were born in 1932 but unfortunately one died before leaving hospital. The other, Betty Kathleen survived. The family lived on Western Road in Leicester.

Their home was a Victorian terraced house with a long alleyway at the back of the houses which gave access to a lot of the homes. The gate to their yard was Audrey's favourite place to sit and watch all of the comings and goings along the alley and in the area. They didn't have a bathroom at that time, just a tin bath hanging out of the way, in the scullery was a copper boiler to heat the water. A kitchen range provided a source of heat and was their means of cooking their food.

Audrey attended Upperton Road Infants School for a year, until the family moved to Bakewell Street in the Highfields area of Leicester. They lived next door to Audrey's maternal grandparents; her grandfather was a police sergeant. She remembers that he was thought to be "very, very fair." In those days the police preferred to "give a clip around the ear" if children were caught misbehaving. It was quite effective!

Audrey attended Melbourne Road Infants School. She remembers that one of her teachers, Miss Oldacre, spoke to Audrey's Mum to tell her that she had asked Audrey "does your tongue never ache?" to which Audrey replied by sticking her tongue out and wiggling it before saying "No"! (Quite a chatterbox then.) Audrey moved to Charnwood Street Junior School where she met her long-time friend, Vera Wilson and a girl called Mary Ansell. Following this she attended Melbourne Road School again until she left at 14. During this time her teachers included the Headmistress, Miss Sarson; her form teacher, Miss Bennett and for her favourite subject of History she was taught by Miss Bailey.

Audrey's father, James died aged 39 in 1941. He was an only child so Audrey had no other family from the Langtons.

When Audrey was 11 years old, in December 1939 she was rushed to hospital and underwent an emergency operation on her appendix. Clearly a very memorable event in her young life.
Upon leaving school Audrey worked in the offices of Graham Gardner, a school uniform manufacturer.

Audrey did shorthand typing and bookkeeping. She really enjoyed the job and stayed for ten years. She only left in 1952, because she was pregnant.

Audrey remembers going to the cinema with her Mum and sister and especially going to see 'The Sound of Music'. As children they particularly enjoyed the cowboy films such a 'Hop-a-Long Cassidy'.

One of Audrey's neighbours had a mother who lived in Syston. This lady was Aunt to Francis Roy (known as Roy) Wain. Audrey and Roy met in 1945 while he was visiting Syston from his job in the Royal Navy working on minesweepers in Malta. Roy told Audrey that they didn't bother to wear their lifejackets on the way out to destroy mines but if they survived the day then they wore them on the way back to harbour. Roy de-mobbed in 1945 and began work in Syston. Their courtship was helped by Roy cycling to see Audrey from Syston to Leicester three or four times a week. They enjoyed walks or visiting friends and going to the Odeon or Savoy cinemas. Roy eventually worked for Rest Assured, a nationally known bedding company located in Syston at the time, where he was an upholsterer.

On Audrey's 21st birthday Roy proposed to her and when she accepted they went to buy the ring from Kemp's in Leicester. (Now the Leicester Tourist Information Centre, with the Kemp's clock still in place over the door.) They married on 21st July 1951 at St Peter's Church in Highfields, Leicester. The new Mr and Mrs Wain spent their honeymoon in Paignton.

Betty, Gordon, Erica, Groom, Bride, Uncle Fred, Betty.
Betty is a sister-in-law; Gordon is a brother-in-law; Erica, her Dad was billeted with Audrey's family during the war; Uncle Fred was Audrey's Godfather; Betty is Audrey's sister, married to Gordon.

The married couple bought the house next to her Mum (previously her grandparents house). In 1952 a son, Stephen Paul, was born in the City General Hospital. In 1956 Andrew was born, followed by Philip in 1961 and the fourth son, Michael in 1963. In 1965 the family moved to Oadby and Audrey still lives in the family home.

Roy drove large cars such as a Zephyr and Rover to transport all six of the family members and because they owned a caravan. This could be towed to Pentuan Sands, at St. Austell Bay in Cornwall. The family went there for most of their early holidays as it was the favourite with the boys. Starting with an inflatable dingy and then a glass fibre boat, the family enjoyed fishing and caught mackerel which they gutted and cooked for their evening meals.

Audrey, Michael, Andrew, Philip and Stephen.

Audrey and Roy enjoyed dancing and joined a class at Gartree School to learn ballroom dancing. They then went dancing at St. Peter's Church Hall on Saturday evenings. They also joined the Casino on Bond Street in Leicester where they liked to decide how much they could afford to lose and then stop. Sometimes they'd come out on top and sometimes they'd lose. It all balanced out. Audrey's Mum babysat for them to enable them to go out when they needed to have some social time to themselves.

Audrey's sons attended schools in Oadby. The older children, Stephen and Andrew, went to Gartree and then Beauchamp College. Philip attended Sandhurst Street and then moved to Gartree and Beauchamp College. The youngest, Michael was able to go to Brocks Hill Infant and Junior School before attending Gartree and Beauchamp College. Audrey describes her sons as 'good lads'. She is obviously proud of them.

Stephen has married Christine and is step-father to her son Steven. Stephen is now self-employed and has a plumbing and heating business. They also have a son called Brett who has spent 24 years in the Navy. He is married to Natalie and they have a son called Sam.

Andrew is a self-employed builder.

In 1972 Roy became very ill when he was aged about 45 and suffered bad migraines. He developed tonsillitis and although the migraines cleared up he had bronchial asthma and emphysimia. He had worked in the Dunlop factory - previously John Bull – as the foreman of the moulding shop which had a lot of loose dust around the products. It is believed that he had been breathing in the dust and fumes from the rubber products which had caused his respiratory problems.

Roy became a manager at Woolco in Oadby (where ASDA is now). Audrey began work again in 1968 when she joined Roy at Woolco. She remained there until she retired in 1988. At the time there was a pub next to the shop called the 'Swinging Sporran' and they often lunched there when they were stock-taking.

Roy became very ill and Audrey was his carer for the last sixteen years of his life. He died in 1990. Audrey had retired from work aged 60 in 1988.

During her retirement Audrey went on holiday to Menorca where she developed an ear infection. This went undiagnosed and has caused her current deafness. During a holiday in Menorca Audrey also suffered a fall. Whilst walking on rough and stoney ground she fell and broke her arm in four places. She was treated in a private hospital where she received very good treatment. On her return home she attended the Leicester Royal Infirmary where she had to undergo a further two operations.

In 2006 Audrey was diagnosed with Parkinson's Disease. She is determined to continue enjoying her life and she now visits her son, Michael and his wife, every couple of weeks.

Audrey began to visit the Age UK Oadby and Wigston lunch club at St Peter's Church Hall every Monday, Wednesday and Friday visits Age UK Oadby and Wigston. She first met Joyce Halls * there and they have become very close friends. They are now collected each Monday to have lunch at the Age UK Oadby and Wigston Day Centre in Wigston. Audrey enjoys the company of friends as well as not having to prepare the food – or do the washing up. She says that it is something to look forward to on a Sunday evening. "Great, it's Monday tomorrow!"

Thank you Audrey.

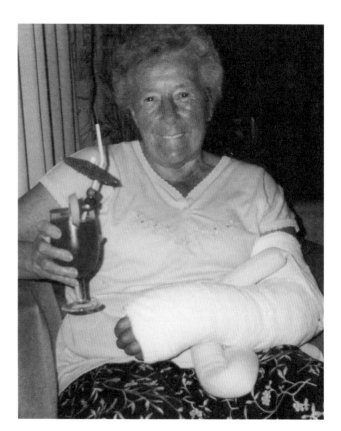

WATERS

Henry Ernest Waters was a "dapper little man" and a member of the Church of England, he married Gertrude Rebecca Yeomans, Barry says that she was a "very tiny lady". She was a Catholic and converted to C of E when they married. Their first child to survive was Maureen born in 1933; the second child is Barry born in 1937; followed by Shirley born in 1939; then Roger born in 1941; Graham was born in 1942; then Barbara in 1944; Terry arrived in 1947; Stuart in 1951; Philip in 1952 and Kevin in 1957. Gertrude had also suffered a number of miscarriages and finally was advised not to get pregnant again.

Barry was born in a house on Gosling Street. The family moved to Napier Street when Barry was one year old. Barry remembers that the milkman used a horse and cart. There was only one car in their street and that was owned by a man who worked for the local government. He attended Hazel Street Primary School and then Lancaster Boys School Secondary School, hating every moment of it. Barry now thinks that he is dyslexic and this explains why he found school so difficult.

Barry remembers that he received a carpentry set for Christmas one year and used it to chop the doors off the doll's house belonging to Maureen. Maureen, Barry and Roger were once scrumping in an orchard on St Mary's Pastures, which was near the Filbert Street area of their home. When a policeman caught them Barry ran off and left Maureen and Roger behind. When he arrived home the policeman was waiting for him. Barry claims that " if you shouldn't do it "– he did! He remembers swimming in the canal because they couldn't afford to go to the swimming baths. Christmas also features in other memories. Most of his presents were made out of wood – a scooter, a car, a train etc. but in 1947 he received an RAF uniform which had a Sam Browne belt and a silver coloured metal pistol. Barry also remembers that one year he was given a pair of slippers and he was very disappointed so he played football in them – they didn't last very long.

Barry and Graham became 'Teddy Boys' as they grew up and Barry was very proud of his hair, he had it cut at Ray's in Jarrom Street on Infirmary Square. He remembers having to pay 6d (approximately 2p) for a Boston and D.A. haircut every week. (This describes a quiff at the front and combing the back to look like a duck's arse, much nicer to call it a D.A.)

Not wanting to continue with school he got a job at 15, knitting at Adley's on Castle Street. The wages at this time were £1 4shillings (approximately £1 30pence) per week. However, a bag of sweets cost 2d and a packet of cigarettes cost 1s (about 10pence). He went through an endless list of jobs including, aged about 16, being an apprentice mechanic at Vaughan Harborn's on Wellington Street in Leicester. He worked on Austin cars and especially the large Austin Princess. Barry believes that his confidence enabled him to get a job really easily. He could leave a job on Friday and get a new one in time to work on Monday. He wasn't "the sharpest tack in the box" but he was very confident and this was his best asset. His longest job was for about twelve months and the shortest for half a day.

When he worked at Swan's on Grasmere Street he left at Monday lunch time and started at D. H. Sam Thompson on the corner of Welford Road and York Road in Leicester, on Tuesday. The factory was a 'Boot and Shoe Mercer', supplying materials to the shoe industry. After Mr D. H. Sam Thompson died the business was sold to a Japanese company. Mr D. H. Sam Thompson is remembered as a "real gentleman". On one occasion Barry had to drive him to the golf club in a big Rover but Barry hadn't driven an automatic car before - Mr D. H. Sam Thompson simply said "You'll soon learn". On another occasion Barry remembers that he accidently ran a dog over. Having killed the dog he wrapped it in a blanket and took it to the police station on Humberstone Road. The owner rang to thank Barry for his care. Barry's last job was as a Hoffman Presser at E. W. Bryan's, on Great Central Street in Leicester, where he stayed until he was forced to retire early with poor health in 1992. The constant breathing in of the fabric dust has caused lung problems.

In 1955 Barry was conscripted into the Royal Leicestershire Regiment to fight against the uprisings in Cyprus, where he served for 2 years earning about £1 7s 6d (about £1 40p). The army paid about £4 5s for being overseas. Before embarking to Cyprus Barry's Dad took him for his first pint. They went to The Bedford pub and he had a Mann's Brown. In Cyprus he drank a spirit beer called 'Keyo' (?) and it "knocked him out" which put him off beer. A Bacardi and coke cost about 1shilling and 3d. (about 15pence).

The regiment left for Cyprus on 5th December 1955, however due to an electrical fault the plane had to land in Malta. Once in Cyprus they marched through the mountains and over golden sands until they finally took an enemy encampment in Famagusta. The regiment began patrol work through rural and urban areas. On his last Friday, before he was due to leave for England, Barry was involved in a very bad lorry accident in which he was thrown through the windscreen and the bonnet flew up to hit him. After two days in hospital Barry insisted he leave hospital despite his condition as he was desperate to go home, an action he somewhat regrets as he gave up a possible six months in the sunshine to get home. His mates in the army thought that he was dead and they threw all of his kit away so he eventually travelled home in borrowed clothes.

Barry received a medal for his service to the UK, and though his regiment lost men he remains extremely proud to have served. He says that his time there was quite "holiday like", as it was about 20% fear and 80% foreign adventure. For the last 30 years he has attended the reunions where they go for a meal and have a service at the church, from where they proudly march to the Town Hall, which is attended by many dignitaries.

In 1958 at a skating rink, Barry met his wife Anne. While showing off Barry had his hands in his pockets and tried to jump over the board around the rink, as he did he caught his skates on the board and tumbled over it. Though he was physically fine, he says his pride was severely damaged. Barry's friend Stan said he would go and talk to her for him, and Barry strictly told him not to so Stan went with all haste and told Anne his friend fancied her. They were going to go to the pub for a pint, but she had gone so he chased her home. They soon found out that Barry's Mum and Anne's Mum knew each other. Anne had gone to school at the same time as Barry's brother but they didn't meet then.

On one occasion when they were skating at the Kettering Drill Hall Barry wore a vivid blue 'Teddy Boy' suit with a shawl collar, and Anne split her jeans whilst skating so had to wear Barry's coat to come home on the train. After courting for three years they were married on 7th October 1961. For their 40th Wedding anniversary Barry an Anne went to Cyprus so that Barry could visit the areas where he worked. He found that to visit the cemetery he would need the permission of the United Nations. However, there is now a memorial to the fallen soldiers at Kyrenia.

Barry and Anne had two sons; Garry who was born in 1962 and Richard who was born in 1967. He watched Richard being born which was unusual at that time. The nurse said half way through that they had a girl, but then out came a very, very pretty boy.

At 13 Richard was involved in a hit and run accident on Cornwell Road. Barry was painting the outside of their home at the time, and his friend ran up to him and told him that Richard had been in a serious accident. Barry jumped from the scaffolding and refused a taxi choosing to run to Cornwell Road. When he reached Richard he believes that he was still breathing and he told him to hang on. When the ambulance arrived they worked on him for a while in the ambulance and Barry followed in a police car. However when they arrived at the hospital the doctors said he must have died instantly. They never did find who was responsible. This changed Barry and his family forever. In attempts to feel better they ended up wasting a lot of their savings, and Barry even says he became suicidal for around 2 years. He says that without a doubt though, what got him through it was his wife Anne, and by sticking together they overcame their troubles. They kept Richard's football kit, his cub's uniform, his favourite denim jacket and all of his photos, books and school reports.

Garry was completely different to Richard. One night, aged 14 he got home at midnight, and Barry said they had their only 'talk' where they both became very emotional and after which Garry agreed to be home at 9pm. One night Barry got a 'phone call from Garry saying his bike had frozen up and he was going to be late home, so Barry told him he had better put his bike on his shoulder and start walking, Garry arrived home at 9.10pm! Their relationship has always been very strong and Garry once told his father that the only thing he ever held against his Dad was that he refused to buy him a Chopper bicycle when he was younger.

Garry married Jo in 1988 and has two sons; Ben born in 1991, and Jonathan born in 1994. Barry thinks that he looks like a character in Scooby Doo as he has red hair and a goatee beard so this is now his nickname, as least as far as Barry is concerned.

Garry got a job at Wyko Bearings and Transmissions, now Eric's a Norwegian company in Derby, where he worked his way up to a managerial job and still works there now. Every year he receives a bonus, and one day told Barry he was using his bonus to take his parents to Florida. Anne dragged Barry around the whole amusement park, despite him having angina. Jonathan was taken to Cape Canaveral for his birthday and he became very interested in learning to fly. He now works with his Dad and delivers their products as well as undertaking sales.

When Barry and Anne were both retired in 2006, she and Barry began to volunteer at Age Concern – now Age UK Oadby and Wigston. Barry began by driving the mini-bus, then as an escort on the bus. He has worked in the coffee shop and now works in the Elderberries unit for the frail and elderly. He still enjoys having a coffee or lunch and spending time socialising with friends at the centre. They are both very valuable volunteers and have been recognised for the work that they do "over and above" the usual time commitment.

Barry and Anne attended a presentation dinner to honour the work that Anne has done for Age UK Oadby and Wigston. We are very grateful for everything that they do.

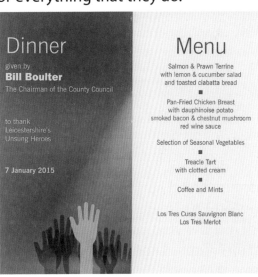

Dinner

given by
Bill Boulter
The Chairman of the County Council

to thank
Leicestershire's
Unsung Heroes

7 January 2015

Menu

Salmon & Prawn Terrine
with lemon & cucumber salad
and toasted ciabatta bread

Pan-Fried Chicken Breast
with dauphinoise potato
smoked bacon & chestnut mushroom
red wine sauce

Selection of Seasonal Vegetables

Treacle Tart
with clotted cream

Coffee and Mints

Los Tres Curas Sauvignon Blanc
Los Tres Merlot

TERRY
WARNER

Terry was born on 18th January 1933, in Leicester. His parents were William Edward (Ted) Warner and Phyllis, nee Peet. They were married after having to fight a court case to be able to marry as Phyllis's mother didn't want her to marry Ted. Terry was the eldest child, he had three brothers – Ron, Brian and Ray. Ron married Amy and had Tony and Marie, who now lives in Skegness. Brian married another Marie and they had Russell, who now lives in Australia and Dawn. Ray married Brenda and they had four children, a boy who has since died and a girl, Helen and twins Derek and Graham.

Terry remembers that during the war, when he was 6, the family sheltered under the stairs at home as his mother didn't like the community shelter, she thought they would be safer at home.

Terry went to school in South Wigston, at the High School. He remembers that Mrs Hall was a support in most of his lessons.

He left school at 14 and went to work in a hosiery factory which was on Bond Street in Leicester. Mr Davis was the boss and Terry learnt to be a knitter. His wages at this time were about £1.45d per week. (£1 and approximately 40p today) He gave his Mum £1 and had the 45d to himself. Eventually Terry decided that he could earn more money if he left, so at the age of 18 he went to work as a builder's labourer for Laing's builders, not only did he earn more but he got bonus's as well. Houses in Eyres Monsell, Thurnby Lodge and Scraptoft were built with Terry's help and he's very proud to see this part of his history.

In 1958, when he was 25 Terry met a girl and they moved to Peterborough. They came back to Leicester when she became pregnant and their sons Alan, Peter and David were born. They separated in 1964.

Terry worked as a machine setter at Parmeko on West Avenue in Wigston for 16 years, until they closed down. During this time Terry was invited by his mates to go to the Working Men's Club in Syston where he met Lyenette. They married and had Jane, John and Steven. At this time the family lived on Holmden Avenue. They owned a Ford car and travelled to Margate for the family holidays for quite a few years. Terry now has three grandchildren. John's children are Leo and Rosie and Jane's child is William. Steven is now married to Zoe and they both enjoy motorbikes. In 2014 Steven won national recognition and was featured in the Leicester Mercury . Zoe has also performed a parachute jump and is now learning to become a pilot.

Steve wheelie is a world beater!

PICTURE: ARON VICKERS PHOTOGRAPHY
UP, UP AND AWAY: Steve Warner performing at the World Wheelie Championships

by **FIONA DRYDEN**

you have ever pulled a wheelie on your bicycle and been proud of your achievement, just imagine how Steve Warner feels.

The mechanical engineer, from Enderby, has clinched the world record for the fastest run wheelie on a non-turbo motorbike – after reaching 190.6mph on his BMW 1000RR.

The 36-year-old beat the record of 180mph last weekend at the World Wheelie Championships despite difficult weather conditions, including 20mph side winds.

Steve said: "I had good runs all weekend, but couldn't crack 170mph.

"The event was paused on Sunday due to high winds and after it restarted I had one

my time was confirmed – a world record for a non-turbo bike."

The World Wheelie Championships, run by Straightliners, are held each year at Elvington Airfield, outside York.

This was Steve's fourth year of competing, having previously achieved a personal best of 159mph.

He said: "It's a difficult thing to sustain a wheelie over an entire kilometre.

"You have to make sure you get your balance right and it helps if the weather isn't against you.

"I had one last crack at it and thankfully I got a good speed."

Steve was up against about 30 other motorcyclists from around the world, competing across various categories.

He came fourth overall in the

the event was set by Egbert Van Popta, from Holland, on his Hayabusa 1300. He reached 199.4 mph, also setting a new world record.

Steve said: "It's lots of fun and you get to meet some brilliant people.

"I never thought I'd be good enough to compete, but I just kept practising and practising until I reached a certain level and my confidence had grown enough to take part.

"I'll keep going each year just to try and better my results and put my skills to the test.

"I first got into motorbikes when I was 17 and realised it was ridiculously expensive to insure a car, and ever since then it's been a huge passion of mine."

ON TRACK TO SUCCESS

Reproduced by kind permission of the Leicester Mercury.

Having left Parmeko Terry worked for Premier Drum and remained there until he was 75. However he really enjoys retirement and "doing nothing". He spent some time visiting the Cafe in the Co-operative shop on Bell Street and there he met Kath Carver*.

Kath persuaded him to visit Age Concern with her and in about 2011 he began to pop in for a coffee and a chat. After approximately two years Terry and his 'new' friends, Mary H., Shirley and Anne, went on holiday together to Babbacoombe. It was strictly for the company and even though there were double beds available everyone behaved themselves properly! Terry didn't go on the day trips with them as he preferred to go off on his own to explore the countryside.

See chapter on Kathleen Carver.

Terry moved from his big family home, which was difficult to heat, to a flat in Peardon Court. This is "very, very nice" as it is warm and comfortable. Although it is taking Terry some time to get used to an electric cooker, he says that he "should have done it a long time ago." He is able to prepare hot meals every evening and enjoys fish and meat pies so he is learning to deal with the cooker.

He still likes to visit Age UK Oadby and Wigston for coffee and snacks and to meet his friends for a chat.

In 2015 Terry was diagnosed with prostate cancer. He has coped with the treatment quite well but has ups and downs. When he was first diagnosed he got all of his family together and told them that he was going to "live with it". When he was quite poorly over Christmas 2015 his family supported him and helped him to recover.

Terry enjoys his social life at Age UK Oadby and Wigston and especially as his friends are mostly 'the girls' in the corner!

GLENYS
WILKINSON

Glenys was born on 13th February 1932 at home in Curzon Street. Her parents were Albert Dilkes and Catherine nee Smith. Glenys is the eighth of their sixteen children. *(see chapter on Eileen Toach)*

The midwife who delivered Glenys was Nurse Dobson and was Welsh. Her name was Glenys. She greeted the new baby by saying "not very pretty but will be intelligent". The nickname by which Glenys was known at home is 'Tragedy Queen' as her Dad used to say that she was "always making things hard".

At the age of five Glenys attended the Knighton Fields Road School. She then went to Holy Cross Catholic School where she sat the 11+ examination and having passed she was awarded a scholarship to Alderman Newton Girls' School. Glenys remembers the Headmistress was called Miss Pedley and she is described as "a strict discipliarian". Glenys's older sister, Eileen was a dressmaker and was able to make school blouses for Glenys. Her friends were Audrey Coltman and Pamela Nutt. Pamela's nickname was 'Peanut'. Audrey is now married and called Audrey Rowley and the two friends still meet.

Glenys wore her hair in ringlets and she remembers standing at the kitchen sink and her Mum would wrap Glenys's hair around her fingers after wetting it with cold water.

When she left school Glenys worked at Lewis's. (Not to be confused with John Lewis. This was in a building where the Marks and Spencer entrance is on Humberstone Gate.) After a trial period on the shop floor she worked in the accounts office. One of her memories is of the tube system which carried the cash from the sales counters to the offices upstairs. These were operated by suction pulling the tubes around the shop. Glenys earned £2.10shillings per week (£2.50) and was trained in book-keeping as well as shorthand and typing skills. This was a very good job and she stayed for a long time because it was "really nice". Different classes were offered to the staff to broaden their education. Mr Sutton was Glenys's boss at the time and she describes him as "really kind".

Glenys often went to the Knighton Fields Road School Youth Club and she enjoyed being a bit "flirty" and had "lots of boyfriends". When she was about 17 or 18 – about 1949 or 1950 - she met a man called Derek Wilkinson at a Parish Room Dance Hall where she went on Saturday nights. Derek was an apprentice in electrical engineering and didn't earn very much so Glenys often paid for their dates.

Derek joined the Army for his National Service and became a Corporal in the Signals. He also had a loud voice and it was very useful when he became a drill instructor.

They were married on 4th July 1953 at St James's Church on Lansdowne Road in Aylestone. The church is no longer there. Glenys wore a dress which had become a "family heirloom" and she carried a bouquet of pink carnations. Her sister Beryl was the Maid of Honour and wore a pink and blue cotton dress, her sister Betty and her cousin Brenda were the bridesmaids and they wore blue taffetta dresses. All of their dresses were made by her sister Eileen. Derek and Glenys enjoyed a honeymoon in Bournemouth. Derek was a very demonstrative man and enjoyed being able to look after his wife.

After leaving Lewis's Glenys went to work nearer to her home and was employed by a knitwear company called Carter and Burrell on Cavendish Road, as a secretary. They also had a branch on Humberstone Road. The business moved their offices to Abbey Park Road and Glenys had an office to herself with "lovely" views over the Park.

However, Glenys's friend Audrey had married and her husband, Ken and Derek set up their own knitwear business which was called Rowley and Wilkinson situated on Paget Street in Aylestone. Ken was able to continue at work until he was 51 when he died of motor neurone disease. Derek kept the business going until he was 55, when he sold it. Derek was a keen bowler and was the Green Ranger looking after the greens at the Leicester Banks Club in Aylestone.

Derek and Glenys had their first child, a boy called Russell, in February 1959. Their second child, Paul was born in February 1962.

n 1963 the family visited America. They travelled on the Queen Mary to New York where they stayed for five days and then flew to Houston where they lived in Tomball. When they registered as visitors at the British Embassy Glenys was offered a job to work for the Consul at the British Embassy. Glenys was to be covering the job of another woman who was on compassionate leave.

I Glenys was required to sign the Official Secrets Act and still doesn't talk about her work there. Her 28 year old brother Ray lived nearby so he and his new wife Pam, looked after Glenys's children whilst she went to work part-time and Derek worked as an electrician. The family didn't settle as their family ties in England were too strong. Their return to England was on 22nd November 1963, the day that President John Kennedy was shot. Glenys and Derek heard the news when they were visiting the Empire State Building before flying home. Glenys remembers that everyone else was crying about the assassination and this has clearly stayed in her memory.

On their return to England they moved in to a house on Castleton Road in Wigston and Glenys began to work as the secretary to Mr Osbourne at F.U.London on Gloucester Crescent in Wigston. Mr Osbourne was a very kind employer and treated Glenys very well. The company moved to Whetstone and one of the van drivers gave her a lift to work as it was not easy to get to from Wigston. Glenys then moved to work at D.E.Sharp on Pullman Road in Wigston. Her boss was John Sharp and his father was called Dennis. Dennis was "a lovely man" and was the Chairman of Leicester City Football Club. Glenys worked for four mornings per week and made lots of friends whilst she was there. One of the most important is still her friend, Christine Leedham. Glenys retired in 1991.

Derek and Glenys's son Paul has married Bridget and they have two sons. Glenys's grandchildren are Joseph born in 1992 and William born in 1996.

Russell, the eldest of Glenys's children is now married to Eileen.

In 2014 Derek died aged 82 of a brain tumour and Glenys didn't like being on her own. She felt that she needed something to do. She is a member of the Ladies Fellowship Group at the Methodist Church in Wigston. She also visited Age Concern on Paddock Street. Glenys decided to volunteer there and has worked on reception for 20 years as the Monday morning volunteer although she also works extra hours when needed. Volunteering at Age UK Oadby and Wigston on Paddock Street has "really enriched my life" and she would recommend it to "anyone looking for something to do and to find new people to meet".

Glenys has described many people in her life as "lovely people" but it seems to me that she is the lovely one. I believe that it is Glenys who has enriched our lives. Thank you.

MARY
WILLIAMS

Mary was born to Gerald Gilbert Basford and Lillian (nee Slater) on 9th December 1926. The family lived in a bungalow in the grounds of Knighton Hall. Mary's father was a mechanic for much of his early life and then went on to be a chauffeur for Bob Gerard's mother and a bus driver for the remainder of his time.

He also drove for Bob Gerard Racing Cars. Mary's mother was a cook before she married and had her children. Mary had two brothers, Joe and Gilbert, Mary also had a younger sister Peggy, who was just 15 months younger than her and also her best friend. Mary and her family moved house as their bungalow became too small for their relatively large family. Her mother was a housewife for the family in their Clarendon Park home which Mary described as "small, nice and warm, just a lovely home" where they were "very happy, all of us together".

Mary attended Sir Jonathan North High School when it first opened and she left at the age of 14. She went straight into full time work in the Wheatsheaf Shoe Factory. The factory was close to home and Mary really did enjoy her job.

Her role was to stamp 'utility' on the soles of the shoes. Mary remembers that when she got her first wage packet she ran all the way home to give the money to her Mum. This is where, aged 16, she met her greatest love, Vic Williams. Vic was born on11th October 1925 and had a twin brother called Edward, known as Ted.* Vic was a clicker at the same shoe factory. In her words, it was 'love at first sight'.

Vic volunteered for the Navy aged 17 ½ and was sent out to America to meet his ship, HMS Foley. When in America, he would write letters and poems to her. One poem that has stayed in her heart is:

"Think of me when this you see, Although we're miles apart,
Others will have my company, But you will always have my heart".

They married when Mary was 21 on 4th February 1947 in the local registry office. Mary wore a brown suit and hat. Mary and Vic couldn't afford a honeymoon at the time but have since enjoyed many family holidays. The couple went on to have three sons; Michael, John and Tony respectively. The family lived in rooms in the Clarendon Park area before moving to a house in Wigston. After their first child Michael was born, Mary became a housewife and Vic had left the navy and went back to clicking in the same shoe factory.

He eventually went into working in insurance. He needed to use his mental arithmatic skills when working with the clients in their homes. As a family, Mary and Vic used to go on family caravan holidays to Chapel St Leonards and Torquay. Mary described her children as always being 'good lads'. However she does remember one holiday when Vic went swimming in the sea in Devon, and 'lost' his swimming trunks! Luckily he managed to get them back on before getting out of the water. John loved the sea and his Grandad took him swimming. It became such a regular event that one day, just after they had arrived on the beach, Grandad looked around and John was stripped off and ready to get in the water.(We will spare John's blushes as to whether he had any swimming trunks on!) When the boys left home Mary and Vic still drove down to Torquay for their holidays as it was Vic's home. They did have one holiday in Australia as Vic's brothers lived there. Mary also recalls a holiday in Paris. Having arrived at the hotel and as they were being shown their rooms, Mary needed to use the bathroom.

* See Kathleen Carver interview.

She went in to the first room next door and found a naked man in the bath. Mary was very embarrassed and hoped that she wouldn't meet him at breakfast! (There seems to be a theme of nakedness in this life history!)

Michael is married to Marie and they have two children, Lisa and Jordan who are both in their 30's. Jordan is married to Leila and they have two children, Spencer and Holly. Jordan works with the police. Leila also works with the police. Michael worked in local government for some time and proudly met Prince Phillip and the Queen. He now works for the NHS and met Prince Charles and his wife, Camilla when the Royal couple visited a hospital in Cornwall.

John worked as a car mechanic. John is married to Chris and they have two daughters who are in their 30's, Hayley and Gemma. John's girls are both very involved with charities and love helping out. Hayley enjoys painting and making jewellery and cards. Hayley is married to Nigel and they have a son called Zak. Gemma is married to Jonathan and works as a charity fundraiser. John now owns his own car sales business in Wigston called Bishop and Bishop.

Tony is married to Angela and they also have two children, Nathan and Daniel and they are both in their 20's. Tony began his working life in printing. He then went back to college and qualified to teach management courses. He is now able to assess management examinations. Nathan is a sports and maths teacher and his partner, Charlotte is also a teacher of sports. Daniel qualified in his Graphics design course with a First Class Degree. His long term girlfriend, Grace is to teach in a local primary school. Daniel now works as a graphic designer in Leicester. Mary is very proud of her grandchildren, she said there are many "never ending stories" about them. She sees all her grandchildren regularly. She also loves having great grandchildren. Mary and Vic moved to a bungalow in 1995 when Vic became ill and they needed a smaller home. Vic sadly died in November 2001.

Tony and Angela, Nathan and Charlotte, Grace and Dan

John and Chris, Hayley and Gemma

Tony, Angela, Nathan, Charlotte, Grace, Dan and Mary.

Mary enjoys gardening, cleaning, washing and entertaining and throwing dinner parties in her Little Hill home where she has been living for over 20 years now. She has recently undergone operations on her cataracts and is looking forward to being able to see more clearly with both eyes. Mary visits Age UK Oadby and Wigston 3 or 4 times a week and spends the day with her friends and having lunch.

She also enjoys organising weekly, Thursday shopping trips with her friends using the 'Friendly Five' mini-bus. The driver, Richard takes them to various shopping centres around Leicestershire and they have visited Loughborough, Market Harborough and as far away as Nuneaton. Mary collects the money for the trip and she asks where they all want to go and then she lets Richard know what his instructions are.
(I can easily see Mary organising everyone!)

Appendix A - Charity Time Line
Appendix B - Interviewers questionaires

Appendix A

Time line for Age UK Oadby and Wigston

2nd November 1964	General Purposes Sub-Committee of Wigston District Council agreed to survey the needs of local people.	Chairman – Dr. N.G. Reynolds
17th November 1964	General Purposes Sub-Committee in favour of the formation of a Wigston Old People's Association.	Chairman – Dr. N.G. Reynolds Present – Mr R.C. Weston Mrs M.K. Daetwyler
3rd March 1965	Formation of Wigston Old People's Welfare Association.	Chairman – Mr R.C. Weston, Council members and representatives from local organisations.
13th May 1965	Executive Committee appointed.	Hon. Secretary – Miss Margaret Moss
1970	New Chairman.	Mr Alan Kind
1971	National Old People's Welfare Association became known as Age Concern.	
August 1971	First 'Contact Centre', serving refreshments, opened in South Wigston Methodist Church. Open Monday and Thursday 10am -12pm.	

17th May 1972	The minutes of the Executive Committee record the change of name to Age Concern.	
1972	Lease agreed on 46 Long Street, above the Oadby and Wigston Advertiser Offices.	
1973	Luncheon Club starts at the Church each Saturday. Transport in a mini-bus being provided where needed.	
9th January 1973	Possibility of land for purchase on Paddock Street. Council agrees to reserve land for a drop-in centre.	
22nd March 1973	Planning application submitted.	
26th June 1973	Planning consent granted.	

September 1974	Further 'Drop In' Centre at The Poplars in Wigston Fields opened.	
18th December 1974	Name officially changed to Age Concern.	
April 1975	Another 'Drop In' Centre at The United Reform Church in Long Street opened.	
19th June 1975	Help The Aged gave £20,000.	
August 1975	Appointment of a 'Neighbourly Help Organiser' to visit those in need. A grant from the Borough Council supported the post.	Mrs Marjorie Robson
29th August 1975	Borough Council wanted to get money for the Centre by diverting funds from bus token vouchers-The Trustees of Age Concern did not agree to this.	

3rd September 1975	Leicester Mercury reported that plans for the centre may have to be shelved because of the economic climate.	
9th January 1976	Leicester City Council agreed to a grant of £7,500 providing work on the centre began within 12 months. They also wanted an undertaking that the Centre would exist for 10 years. At this point in time, the Trustees could not promise this.	
17th March 1976	Draft deed of covenant between Age Concern Wigston and City Council, money to be used solely for the Centre and to be repaid with interest if the centre ceases to exist within 10 years.	
March to April 1976	Disagreements between the Borough Council and the County Council created further delays. The Borough Council asks Age Concern to make a formal approach for the land.	

28th April 1976	Alan Kind wrote to the Council perturbed as to why planning permission was granted in 1973 yet they are only now being asked to make a formal approach.	Letter on file
9th February 1977	Approval finally given for the lease of the land on Paddock Street.	
12th March 1977	The first 'turf' was cut.	Mr John Farr M.P. performed the ceremony. Mayor Walter Boulter was present.
14th March 1977	Contractors arrived on site.	R.C.Weston & Son
14th May 1977	Launch of 'Buy a Brick' campaign.	Larry Grayson and David Hobman, Director of Age Concern England present.

22nd June 1977	The lease is agreed. Age Concern will pay the Borough Council £25.00 rent for 35 years.	
3rd January 1978	The 'Neighbourly Help Service' moved into the new building.	
2nd October 1978	The shop is opened.	
25th April 1978	The car park is completed.	Management Sub-Committee minutes.
15th September 1979	Official opening of the centre.	Sir Alan Marre KCB, Chairman of Age Concern, England performed the ceremony.
30th November 1979	The land becoming freehold via a payment of £2,000 to the Borough Council was discussed.	Management Sub-Committee minutes.
20th December 1979	This is agreed with the proviso that the Council can purchase the building and the plot, should Age Concern wish to sell in the future.	Management Sub-Committee minutes.

17th March 1981	Planning permission was given to extend the building.	
18th September 1981	The extension had been agreed and the Health Authority had given permission for Age Concern to have access via their land whilst the work was done.	
1981	Preparations to extend the building begin.	
8th October 1981	The 'First Turf' cutting performed by the Mayor of Oadby and Wigston.	Councillor, Mrs Primrose Wray.
October 1982	Official Opening of the extension performed by the Mayor.	Councillor, Mr Donald Mobbs.
19th January 1983	Appeal launched to buy another mini-bus.	
10th November 1983	The vehicle arrives.	
30th September 1986	Regional health Authority write that we may be able to purchase a small piece of land from them subject to them being able to sell the rest of the land without the portion that Age Concern want	

22nd September 1987	Regional Health Authority offer us a lease for the land which will be for 60 years with a premium payment of £3,500 and thereafter a nominal rent of one peppercorn.	
29th June 1988	The lease is agreed and confirmed to run for 60 years.	
14th October 1988	Bertram Cullum leaves Age Concern in the region of £150,000 in his will.	
5th May 1989	Shop opened where it currently is.	Minutes 22nd May
21st February 1990	A decision is made to provide a service at Bassett Street.	Minutes of the meeting
December 1990	Christmas Eve opening for soup and pudding began.	
8th June 1992	Shop extended	Minutes 8th June
12th December 1994	The Frail Elderly Unit is established now as 'The Elderberries'.	
14th June 1996	First patio garden is opened.	

1996-1997	Indoor Bowls began on a Tuesday.	AGM Report
19th March 1997	Area Health Authority states they do not now want any money for the land.	
25th April 1997	Plans for the garage are drawn up.	
22nd May 1997	An application is made for funding towards employing two Neighbourhood Care Officers.	
1997-1998	Scones, sausage rolls and cakes were introduced to the Coffee Bar menu Thursday Indoor Bowling started Watercolour classes began The Walking Group commenced	AGM Minutes 1998

19th June 1998	The Garage is complete.	
14th October 1998	Planning permission granted to extend the building.	
30th October 1998	Alan Kind is awarded an MBE for his service to Age Concern.	
30th September 1999	National Lottery grant is obtained for building extension and the salary of a part-time (6 hours) Development Officer.	
8th June 2000	The Pagoda Turret was ordered.	
30th August 2000	Automatic doors installed.	
2000-2001	Building extended at the front and back to provide disabled toilets, the Maple Room , Hairdressing and Chiropody Room, and offices, a shower room, laundry and First Aid Room.	
24th November 2000	Maple Room officially opened.	

2006	Regrettably our operation at Bassett Street in South Wigston proved unsustainable. The clients are brought to Paddock Street.	
July 2007	The Maud Elkington Trust gave Age Concern Oadby and Wigston £7,500 towards a new converted minibus with the proviso that the rest of the money is raised by Christmas 2007.	
Christmas 2007	The generosity of service users and the local community help us realize our dream of a new vehicle. One person donated £5,000. The Peugeot was purchased in 2008.	
2008	Lottery money paid for refurbishment of the coffee bar.	
31st October 2008	30 years celebration at Paddock Street.	

August 2009	The kitchen is fully refurbished with grants from two charitable trusts:- The Countess Eleanor Peel and The Clothworker's Foundation. A legacy and a grant from the Garfield Weston Foundation ensured we had our windows double glazed. Cooked snacks from the Coffee Bar began.	AGM 2010
2011-2012	Refurbishment for the dining room was completed with a grant from the Borough Council. They also granted us the money to purchase our leased minibus. Oadby Rotary paid for a new Bowls Mat	Work of the Centres Booklet.
June 2012	The name became Age UK Oadby and Wigston.	

January 2014	Projector Screen installed, paid for by the Wigston Greater Historical Society.	
8th August 2014	Oadby forced to close because of high rents. St Peter's Church takes over running of the lunch club and staff are retained there.	
20th February 2015	The Sensory Garden is completed funded by The Lottery and the County Council.	
24th February 2015	We were assessed by outside assessors employed by Age UK nationally to check out that we run properly. We passed with flying colours.	
26th June 2015	A full day of celebrations for the 50th Anniversary	

Interviewers questionnaires

Information from students who helped with the interviews for the Memories book

Why did you volunteer to help with this project?
At first it was only a Uni assignment but I quickly got engaged in it! It is good to help in such a great project. I am happy to be part of it!

How did you think that it would benefit you?
I became more sensitive (knowing people's stories) and had a desire to know some bits of Leicester's history. I met Anne, a great person!

What were your feelings before you visited the Day Centre for the first time. Were you nervous or worried about meeting the older people?
I was stressed before meeting an Age UK representative because I didn't know what to expect. How difficult would be the part of the work that we would do. I haven't visited the Day Centre yet.

How would you describe the experience of interviewing the older people? Did anything surprise you, worry you or make you uncomfortable?
I didn't interview people but worked on the appearance of the interviews. They were very funny and motivating. I loved Ray's interview – he's such a creative person, loved his 'Ode'.!

Did you enjoy the stories that you heard? Did you learn anything?
Oh yeah! Life can be hard but we always need to think positively!

Would you like to volunteer in the future? Either with us or with any other charity?
Why not…

Do you have any other comments to make?

Thank you for all of your help,
Anne

Information from students who helped with the interviews for the Memories book

Why did you volunteer to help with this project?
I volunteered to help with this project as part of my Duke of Edinburgh's Award. For the Award it is compulsory to do some voluntary work – I decided Age UK would be the best place to volunteer and was very pleased to hear the project we would be helping with.

How did you think that it would benefit you?
Before starting the project I thought it would help me to become more confident when approaching people and interacting with them. I also thought it would help me become more familiar with people from a different generation from me and understand different generations more as I never usually socialise with anyone out of my own age range.

What were your feelings before you visited the Day Centre for the first time. Were you nervous or worried about meeting the older people?
Visiting the Day Centre for the first time I was slightly nervous. It was a totally new environment and I wasn't sure how to conduct myself. I was also apprehensive about meeting the older people as most people tend to stereotype teenagers as troublesome and I didn't want to create that impression. However, we managed to prove to everyone at the Day Centre that we had good intentions and weren't there to misbehave!

How would you describe the experience of interviewing the older people? Did anything surprise you, worry you or make you uncomfortable?
I definitely enjoyed the experience of interviewing the older people. It was all very new for me and I wasn't quite sure how to go about it, but I think I managed well the first time and gradually became more comfortable as I got to know everyone. I was quite surprised by how relaxed everyone was and how much they all loved a joke. As a teenager I wouldn't expect that but they were just like us in many ways where humour was concerned!

Did you enjoy the stories that you heard? Did you learn anything?
I found most of the stories I heard very interesting, especially hearing about transformations during WWII. It was also really nice to listen to the interviewees talk about their life and see what they had achieved.

Would you like to volunteer in the future? Either with us or with any other charity?
I think I would definitely consider volunteering again, perhaps with Age UK or a different charity. It is really nice to give up your free time to do something for other people and also enjoy yourself while you do it.

Would you recommend volunteering to anyone else?
I would recommend volunteering to other people. While many people may be discouraged to do it knowing they will not be paid I think it is a great way to give up your free time. While you don't gain money I think you gain so much more from volunteering which you cannot put a price on and I definitely think it is something worth doing.

Do you have any other comments to make?
I would like to thank Age UK for allowing me to volunteer for them I had a great time while volunteering and really feel I was made welcome by everyone. I would also like to thank everyone at the Day Centre who was interviews and therefore helped to make the book what it is. It was really nice to feel comfortable during my time at Age UK and I am really pleased I chose that charity to volunteer for.

Thank you for all of your help.
Anne

Information from students who helped with the interviews for the Memories book

Why did you volunteer to help with this project?
The project was brought to my design course group and was offered as a live brief. It was a very interesting project idea and I was keen to do something creative to help a very worthwhile charity.

How did you think that it would benefit you?
I knew that I would have the opportunity to read personal accounts from a variety of older members of the community and was really interested in reading these memories. I was also excited to produce a book cover to help to publish them.

What were your feelings before you visited the Day Centre for the first time. Were you nervous or worried about meeting the older people?
Unfortunately I didn't get to visit the Centre

How would you describe the experience of interviewing the older people? Did anything surprise you, worry you or make you uncomfortable?
N/A

Did you enjoy the stories that you heard? Did you learn anything?
Yes, very much. Life was very different and it was great to read about strong women in a very 'man's world' of the time.

Would you like to volunteer in the future? Either with us or any other charity?
I would love to help again with any creative design work.

Do you have any other comments to make?
I look forward to seeing the completed project when it is published.

Thank you for all of your help.
Anne

Information from students who helped with the interviews for the Memories book
Why did you volunteer to help with this project?
Voluntary work was mandatory for my Duke of Edinburgh Bronze Award and we all decided to volunteer at Age concern. I was very happy with this choice and to come to help around the centre.

How did you think that it would benefit you?
It benefitted me in the way that now I have more knowledge of Wigston and Oadby and how it was in the last century. And on top of that I think having volunteered at age concern would appeal to managers later when applying for a job.

What were your feelings before you visited the Day Centre for the first time. Were you nervous or worried about meeting the older people?
When we went over to interview them I did feel nervous to talk to older people because I didn't want to make a bad approach and scare them.

How would you describe the experience of interviewing the older people? Did anything surprise you, worry you or make you uncomfortable?
As I said I was really nervous when I was about to speak to them but once the conversation started I was really comfortable and I would like to think that they felt the same way. I was really surprised with how they remembered what happened so long ago and in so much detail.

Did you enjoy the stories that you heard? Did you learn anything?
I definitely enjoyed the stories that they told because we were told how it was during the war and what each of them have been through in their life which was really interesting. We also found out how Wigston and Oadby looked like almost a century ago.

Would you like to volunteer in the future? Either with us or with any other charity?
After I have finished with my GCSE's I would love to either come back or do some more voluntary work elsewhere. I think having done volunteering it is a good experience and I would like to do it again.

Would you recommend volunteering to anyone else?

Yes, I think this was a really good experience and I think that I have learnt a lot. I think that my communication skills have improved and having to speak to older people really interested me. I would definitely recommend volunteering at Age Concern to my friends and I think it would be good for them as it was for me.

Do you have any other comments to make?

I am very grateful for being given this opportunity to have helped out as it has given me an experience that I will not forget; and I hope that I was helpful towards the project. Thank you again for having given me this opportunity.

Thank you for all of your help.
Anne

Information from students who helped with the interviews for the Memories book

Why did you volunteer to help with this project?

I volunteered to help with this project as part of my Duke of Edinburgh's Bronze Award. As part of this award it is necessary to do some voluntary work in an optional field. With a few friends I decided that Age UK would be a great place to go and I was delighted when being told the project we were to participate in.

How did you think that it would benefit you?

As the project involved me interacting with other people I thought that this would help me feel more confident and comfortable talking to and around an elder age group. As well as improving my social skills I thought that the project would also help me with my writing and compiling skills as the end aim of the project was to put together a range of memories and views of Wigston.

What were your feelings before you visited the Day Centre for the first time. Were you nervous or worried about meeting the older people?

Before visiting the Day Centre I was extremely nervous. I was unsure on how to conduct myself and act as it was an environment I was not very familiar with. My biggest worry however was interacting with the older people as I was anxious whether I spoke or acted in an acceptable manner. However, within the first half an hour I was confortable and engaged in many conversations with them.

How would you describe the experience of interviewing the older people? Did anything surprise you, worry you or make you uncomfortable?

It was a privilege in many ways interviewing everyone s they were very open and made me feel comfortable when around them. It was an extremely enjoyable and interesting experience as it was very new for me, however, as I got to know everyone it became clear that they were just like us and always loved to throw in a bit of humour!

Did you enjoy the stories that you heard? Did you learn anything?

On interviewing the older people I was fascinated with the memories they have and how clearly they remember events that occurred such a long time ago. The stories that stuck with me the most are the ones based on the war and the things they did to get through as well as the situations they encountered. It was also astonishing hearing about how Wigston has changed. It was also very interesting on hearing the things everyone has accomplished and witnessed throughout their lives.

Would you like to volunteer in the future? Either with us or with any other charity?

I think I would definitely volunteer in the future for Age UK, another charity or an organisation for younger people as it's a great feeling to give up your time and know you're helping someone else.

Would you recommend volunteering to anyone else?

I would certainly recommend voluntary work to all of my friends and family. Despite not getting paid you get so much out of it that you're unlikely to get in a job etc.

Do you have any other comments to make?

I am very grateful for Age UK allowing me to volunteer for them, especially Anne who ensured I was always comfortable and organised the voluntary work. I'd also like to thank everyone that was interviewed and helped us make the book. It was an experience I won't forget and I'm glad I took the opportunity. Thank you very much.

Thank you for all of your help.
Anne

Information from students who helped with the interviews for the Memories book

Why did you volunteer to help with this project?
Been introduced to this project by my tutor and loved the idea of finishing off the project and being part of this.

How did you think that it would benefit you?
I thought it would be interesting to see what this project is about and being part of documenting people's memories.

What were your feelings before you visited the Day Centre for the first time. Were you nervous or worried about meeting the older people?
I didn't visit the Centre

How would you describe the experience of interviewing the older people? Did anything surprise you, worry you or make you uncomfortable?
I did not interview them but putting it all together and reading some of the memories made me happy and interested to find out more.

Did you enjoy the stories that you heard? Did you learn anything?
It was very interesting to read these amazing stories and learn about people and their past and present.

Would you like to volunteer in the future? Either with us or any other charity?
Definitely, if I ever find spare time I would love to do it.
Do you have any other comments to make?

Thank you for all of your help.
Anne

Information from students who helped with the interviews for the Memories book

Why did you volunteer to help with this project?
I volunteered to help with this project because I want to try doing things that I have never tried nor done before. I have always been interested in working and interacting with elders but have not had the chance to do so in the past years. I thought this project would be the perfect opportunity to do so and I enjoyed it very much.

How did you think that it would benefit you?
This project definitely benefits me in various aspects. Firstly, I wanted to study medicine in the future and this opportunity allows me to learn and improve different skills like communication and listening skills, which are very important for doctors. I believe I have gained much more patience and acquired empathy after a few interview sessions when I became more confident with talking to the elders at the Day Centre. Also, spending more time with the elders made me realise the importance of geriatric care. Elders are people like us, but with more experiences in their lives that they want to share with their children and others. The experience made me realise that I actually like establishing interpersonal relationships with others; elders and fellow volunteers alike. I like listening to other people's stories and asking questions to understand more about their lives as well as gaining their trust so that they would become more open and talk more about themselves.

What were your feelings before you visited the Day Centre for the first time. Were you nervous or worried about meeting the older people?
I was extremely nervous because I have never worked nor talked to older people before, let alone foreign older people. I normally feel uneasy and lack confidence when talking to elders because of the very little interaction I have with the elders. The only other people I know are my grandmothers. That is it. I was worried and anxious that I would not understand them or I might appear bored or offensive due to the cultural difference and personality. But after getting to the older people at the Day Centre I realised that my worries and fears were very wrong!

How would you describe the experience of interviewing the older people? Did anything surprise you, worry you or make you uncomfortable?

I would describe the experience of interviewing the older people a very pleasant experience. Not only did I get to hear stories of their lives, which some are very intriguing, I was able to learn more about the British culture as well. Nothing really surprised me or worried me, except for the fact that older people normally live alone in the UK.

Did you enjoy the stories that you heard? Did you learn anything?

I really enjoyed the stories that I heard and learnt quite a few things about the lifestyle of the British people and of their culture way back when.

Would you like to volunteer in the future? Either with us or with any other charity?

I would absolutely like to volunteer to help in the future! Either with you for the project or any other way! Feel free to contact me or get in touch anytime!

Would you recommend volunteering to anyone else?

Yes, definitely!

Do you have any other comments to make?

No.

Thank you for all of your help.
Anne

Information from students who helped with the interviews for the Memories book

Why did you volunteer to help with this project?
I volunteered at Age UK Oadby and Wigston on a 3 month placement to complete the Duke of Edinburgh's Award at bronze level. I wanted to get involved with this project as I believed that there was lots of history behind Wigston and the people within that had been lost or never spoken of. I wanted to participate to unravel this information for the local people to hear about.

How did you think that it would benefit you?
From volunteering at Age UK I thought that I would be able to build my confidence to speak and engage with strangers. I thought that working on the project would improve my research skills but also would allow me to understand the history of Wigston and what actually occurred in the past.

What were your feelings before you visited the Day Centre for the first time. Were you nervous or worried about meeting the older people?
Before I visited the Day Centre for the first time I was extremely nervous but also excited at the same time. It was a new experience so I didn't really know what to expect. I had an idea that it might be quiet and almost restful but it was totally different... All of the people there were talkative , friendly and enthusiastic to help us by giving us the information and memories.

How would you describe the experience of interviewing the older people? Did anything surprise you, worry you or make you uncomfortable?
Interviewing the older people at the Day Centre was very interesting. Everyone was will ing to talk to us and everyone had memories to share. Some of the facts that were told to us were quite surprising but all of the information was intriguing and made you curious to find out more.

Did you enjoy the stories that you heard? Did you learn anything?

I enjoyed listening to all of the stories and memories from the older people. Whether short or long each story was individual and had a lot of history within. I learnt a lot from all of the people at the Day Centre about what Wigston used to be like, major events that occurred and how it had changed from back then.

Would you like to volunteer in the future? Either with us or with any other charity?

I would love to volunteer with either Age UK again or any other organisation to help with projects like this one and events. Volunteering has helped me become more knowledgeable of the lives and needs of others and it has made me realise how important volunteers are to charities and organisations.

Would you recommend volunteering to anyone else?

Volunteering at Age UK Oadby and Wigston was one of the best choices I made. I would recommend it to everyone. It's an experience that builds your confidence and it allows you to see the world from a different perspective. Whether at Age UK or with another organisation I can guarantee that anyone who volunteers will enjoy it and will benefit from it. Even if it's only an hour a week or even an hour a month it will make a difference to your life and the lives of those you help.

Do you have any other comments to make?

I would like to thank Anne and all the staff for taking the time to arrange the placement at Age UK Oadby and Wigston and I would also like to thank all the people at the Day Centre for being so welcoming and inspiring.

Thank you for all of your help.
Anne

Information from students who helped with the interviews for the Memories book

Why did you volunteer to help with this project?
A lot of reasons; firstly it was part of my college brief. I had never designed a book cover before and it was a great opportunity.

How did you think that it would benefit you?
It would work well as part of my portfolio and as a good reference.

What were your feelings before you visited the Day Centre for the first time. Were you nervous or worried about meeting the older people?
I did not visit the centre but I read their stories and they were very interesting and touching.

How would you describe the experience of interviewing the older people? Did anything surprise you, worry you or make you uncomfortable?
It made me value a lot more, hearing their stories.

Did you enjoy the stories that you heard? Did you learn anything?
Yes, I feel like some of them should be published or even made into a film.

Would you like to volunteer in the future? Either with us or with any other charity?
Yes!

Do you have any other comments to make?
Really enjoyed this opportunity and appreciate it a lot.

Thank you for all of your help.
Anne

Information from students who helped with the interviews for the Memories book

Why did you volunteer to help with this project?
The reason is that I'd love to give help to others and especially the elderly people because they really need helping. Doing the memories book is very meaningful and interesting.

How did you think that it would benefit you?
Getting in touch with people will make me more outgoing and mature. It's a good exercise to get a better me in the future.

What were your feelings before you visited the Day Centre for the first time. Were you nervous or worried about meeting the older people?

I was really nervous before I visited the Day Centre for the first time. I don't know how to get contacted with the older people and also worry about our communications if it's comfortable to continue.

How would you describe the experience of interviewing the older people? Did anything surprise you, worry you or make you uncomfortable?
They were all very nice and welcome to me. They were very patient about questions and queries. It's a heart-warming experience. No, not at all.

Did you enjoy the stories that you heard? Did you learn anything?
Yeah, many of those stories that I've never heard before. It was really surprising sometimes. I've learned that nothing was easy for the older people. They had very tough lives when they were young. We should respect them and provide benefits for them.

Would you like to volunteer in the future? Either with us or with any other charity?
Yes, absolutely. I'd love to do this job or anywhere else.

Would you recommend volunteering to anyone else?
Perhaps, I will try my best to find others to volunteer.

Thank you for all of your help.
172 Anne